Basma M.Korany

acupressure as a nursing tool in managing chronic patients

Basma M.Korany

acupressure as a nursing tool in managing chronic patients

Noor Publishing

Imprint
Any brand names and product names mentioned in this book are subject to trademark, brand or patent protection and are trademarks or registered trademarks of their respective holders. The use of brand names, product names, common names, trade names, product descriptions etc. even without a particular marking in this work is in no way to be construed to mean that such names may be regarded as unrestricted in respect of trademark and brand protection legislation and could thus be used by anyone.

Cover image: www.ingimage.com

Publisher:
Noor Publishing
is a trademark of
Dodo Books Indian Ocean Ltd. and OmniScriptum S.R.L publishing group

120 High Road, East Finchley, London, N2 9ED, United Kingdom
Str. Armeneasca 28/1, office 1, Chisinau MD-2012, Republic of Moldova, Europe
Printed at: see last page
ISBN: 978-620-7-47937-5

Introduction

Chronic renal failure (CRF) is one of the main worldwide health problems. In the United States, it is estimated that in the next years, the prevalence of CRF will increase and over two million persons are expected to be receiving renal replacement therapy by 2030. Chronic renal failure induces a slow and progressive decline of kidney function. Furthermore, patients with CRF are complaining of many symptoms such as decreased urination, swelling of legs, puffiness of face, shortness of breath, ammonia breath, nausea and loss of appetite (Abouna, 2020).

In chronic renal failure there is a steady and continued decrease in renal clearance or glomerular filtration rate (GFR), which leads to the accumulation of urea, creatinine and other chemicals substances in the blood that may lead to serious complications such as uremia, anemia, peripheral neuropathy, osteopenia (reduction of bone tissue), fluid overload, congestive heart failure, hypertension, pericarditis, electrolyte imbalances and metabolic acidosis (Jbireal, Azab & Omer, 2020).

Chronic renal failure is associated with increased risks of morbidity and premature mortality. CRF is usually asymptomatic until the end stage (Goldberg & Krause, 2016). End-stage renal disease (ESRD) or the fifth stage of renal failure is an irreversible decline in kidney function in which kidney no longer adequately removes wastes and water from the blood and requires ongoing peritoneal dialysis (PD) or hemodialysis (HD)) or kidney transplantation for survival. Patients on HD account for approximately 92% of the overall dialysis population. Selection of dialysis modality such as HD or PD depends largely upon physician recommendation, patient preference, and the patient's clinical and social status. Most of ESRD patients choose to be placed on lifelong HD machine to sustain life (Hill et al., 2016).

Hemodialysis (HD) is one of the renal replacement therapy. In this technique body waste product like urea, creatinine and free water are removed from the blood; the procedure of hemodialysis is performed two to three times in a week and the time of dialysis is from two to four hours. The time of dialysis depends on various factors, including kidney function, amount of body waste, level of salts and body weight. Furthermore; mortality rate with hemodialysis remains high approximately 18 to 20 percent per year. So, improvements in the technology for dialysis, the development of new pharmaceutical agents, and experience over the course of more than forty years has made maintenance dialysis became available. In addition, HD causes several complications as muscle cramp, pruritus, abdominal pain, hypotension, hypertension, vomiting, short-term weight gain, constipation, chest pain, nausea, anemia, headache, dizziness and sleeping disturbance(Pinheiro, de Macedo & de Carvalho Lira, 2017).

Sleep disturbance (SD) is prevalent in patients with CRF in particular those with end stage renal disease. It has been reported that 44%- 80% of patients with ESRD receiving dialysis report sleep complaints (Danielle, Mahamat, Francois, Marie-Patrice & Gloria, 2017). The different forms of sleep disturbance are rest leg syndrome (RLS), sleep disordered breathing (sleep apnea), excessive day time sleepiness and insomnia (Maung, El Sara, Chapman, Cohen & Cukor, 2016).

Insomnia is considered the major sleep disorder among patients on HD. It is defined as the subjective sensation characterized by one or more of the following symptoms as difficulty falling asleep (sleep onset insomnia), difficulty staying asleep (sleep maintenance insomnia), early morning awakening or poor sleep quality (non-restorative sleep). In most cases, the diagnosis of insomnia is based on the present of these symptoms at least 3 to 4 times a week for several weeks (Hamzi, Hassani, Asseraji & El Kabbaj, 2017).

Insomnia may lead to long and short term consequences. Long term consequences such as hypertension, dyslipidemia, weight-related issues, cardiovascular diseases, metabolic disorders, type 2 diabetes mellitus while short term consequences are: impaired daytime functioning, increase stress responsivity, somatic pain, reduced quality of life, emotional distress, mood, cognitive, memory disorders, performance deficits, fatigue and dizziness(Medic, Wille & Hemels, 2017).

Dizziness is a term used to describe a range of sensations, such as feeling lightheaded, faint, woozy, weak or unsteady and represents 63% of HD patients (Fluck, 2016). There are many causes of dizziness such as insomnia, anemia, low blood pressure and disequilibrium syndrome. There are many consequences of dizziness: short term consequences as increased risk of falling, injury and effect on daily life activities. Long

4

term consequences lead to chronic untreated dizziness (Sattar, Khan, Ahmad, Adnan & Danish, 2016).

Insomnia and dizziness can be treated by pharmacological or non-pharmacological treatment. Pharmacotherapy is associated with abuse, dependence and they have uncertain efficacy with long term use. Limitation of these treatments lead to seeking complementary health approaches (CHAs) to improve sleep and dizziness (Yeung et al., 2018). The most used therapies in CHAs are hydrotherapy, biofeedback, aromatherapy, relaxation technique, massage, acupuncture and acupressure therapy (Bossola et al., 2017).

Acupressure therapy is the fifth most common technique used in CHAs. It is a treatment modality in Traditional Chinese Medicine (TCM) and a non-invasive variant of acupuncture form (Yeung et al., 2018). It is based on stimulation of meridians (a network of energy pathways throughout the body) to increase the flow of energy, subsequently, altering the experience of symptoms. Moreover, it helps to relieve stress, tension, relax muscles and joints, improve sleep, alleviate chronic pain, minimize headache as well treat the symptoms of dizziness by restoring the balance of the energy flow in the body. Hence, it is rapidly gaining acceptance as a safe, cost-effective, non-invasive and non-pharmacological form of therapy (Zeid& Aly, 2020; Mehta, Dhapte, Kadam & Dhapte, 2017).

Nurse working in dialysis units is considered as one of the multidisciplinary team who plays a significant role on reducing insomnia and dizziness levels among patients on hemodialysis by assessing the sleep pattern and quality (sufficient duration; appropriate timing; regularity and absence of sleep disturbance) and assess activity, rest, blood circulation as indicators for dizziness(Taha & Ali, 2015).Actually, it is vital that the nurses pinpoint all factors that may adversely affect the pattern and quality of sleep and determine levels of dizziness for those patients and develop plans to reduce their sleep disorders which by consequently decrease level of dizziness. Also, the nurse should be aware of non-pharmacological therapy such as acupressure to provide proper intervention. Therefore, the aim of the current study is to evaluate the effect of acupressure therapy on insomnia and dizziness among patients undergoing hemodialysis.

Significance of the Study

End Stage Renal Disease is one of the main health problems and its incidence is growing and significantly increased in the developing countries. In Egypt, the estimated annual incidence of ESRD is around 74 per million and the total prevalence of patients on dialysis is 264 per million (El-Arbagy, Yassin, Boshra, 2016). At Kasr El-Aini Hospital, the number of admitted patients having renal failure was 4880, 5230, 5560 patients in 2017, 2018, 2019 respectively. Currently, Nephrology-Dialysis Transplantation Center is serving176 patients (Kasr El-Aini Hospital Medical Records and Statistics Department-Cairo University, 2019).

Scanty researches were conducted aiming to evaluate the effectiveness of acupressure therapy on insomnia and dizziness among patients undergoing hemodialysis.

Moreover, during the investigator clinical experience, these patients verbalized feelings of despair resulting from insomnia in the form of fatigue, irritability, difficulty in concentration and decreased ability to perform activity of daily living while, dizziness is experienced in the form of light headed, feeling faint and drowsiness.

Therefore, this study will build upon the science of complementary therapy which may be useful to nursing and other health care professionals to decrease distress of insomnia and dizziness as well as optimizing quality of care for this group of patients. In addition, it is hoped that the findings of the current study will increase nurse's knowledge related to non-pharmacological management of insomnia and dizziness for patients on hemodialysis that may reflect positively on patients care and economic issues. Also, it is hoped that this effort might generate attention and motivation for further researches in this area of complementary therapy and establish evidence based data that can promote nursing practice and research.

Aim of the Study

The aim of the current study is to evaluate the effect of acupressure therapy on insomnia and dizziness among patients undergoing hemodialysis.

Research Hypotheses

To fulfill the aim of the study, the following research hypotheses were formulated:-

H_1: The study group patients who received acupressure therapy will have significant lower mean insomnia scores than control group who receive routine hospital care.

H_2. The study group patients who received acupressure therapy will have significant lower mean dizziness scores than control group who receive routine hospital care.

Operational Definitions

The following operational definitions were used in this study:

Acupressure therapy is a noninvasive technique performed by the investigator through using tips of fingers to apply pressure and stimulate 8 points right and left along the meridians of the body.

Insomnia is a subjective sensation characterized by one or more of the following symptoms as difficulty falling asleep, difficulty staying asleep, early morning awakening or poor sleep quality and it is measured by insomnia severity index (Thakral, Von Korff, McCurry, Morin& Vitiello, 2020).

Dizziness is a term used to describe a range of sensations, such as feeling light headed, faint, woozy, weak or unsteady and it is measured by dizziness assessment tool that, developed by the investigator in the current study.

Review of Literature

Towards achieve the aim of the current study which was to evaluate the effect of acupressure therapy on insomnia and dizziness among patients undergoing hemodialysis the current study literature review is presented in the following sequences: Anatomy and physiology of the urinary system, an overview of renal failure, pathophysiology, and its classification, medical and nursing management of chronic renal failure. Moreover, the current review represents sleep disturbance, insomnia and dizziness in addition to, an overview about alternative therapy (acupressure therapy).

Anatomy and Physiology of the Urinary System

1-Anatomy of the Kidney

The urinary system consists of two kidneys, two ureters, bladder and urethra (Figure 1). Kidneys are a pair of bean shaped, brownish red structures located behind and outside the peritoneal cavity on the posterior wall of the abdomen from the 12th thoracic vertebra to the3rd lumber vertebra in the adult. Moreover, the right kidney is slightly lower than the left due to the location of the liver and externally, the kidneys are well protected by the ribs and by the muscles of the abdomen and back; internally, fat deposits surround each kidney providing protection for it. Also, the average adult kidney weighs approximately 113 to 170g, 11 to 12 cm long, 5 to 7.5cm wide and 2.5 to3cm thick (Chalmer & Charlotte, 2019).

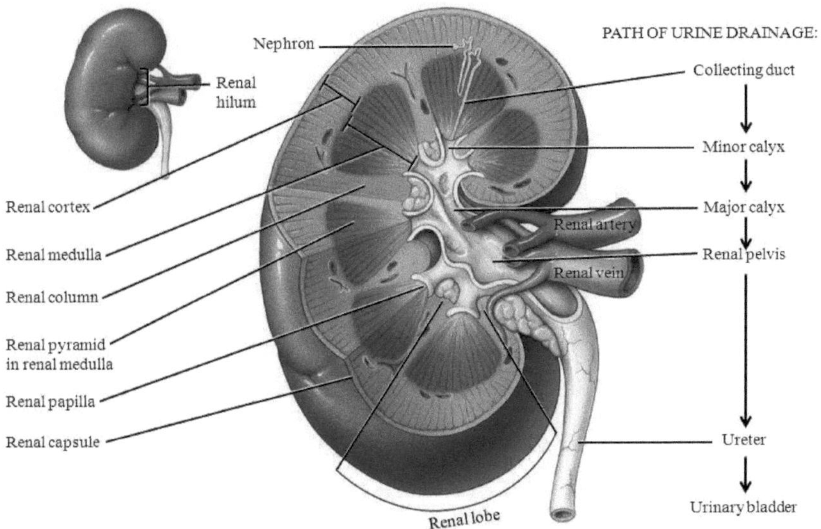

Figure1. Frontal section of the right kidney*: Crisler, Johnston, Sivula & Budelsky, 2020. Functional Anatomy and Physiology In The Laboratory Rat (pp.91-132). Academic Press. available @ https://www.google.com /search?q=Frontal section of the right kidney.*

Additionally, the kidney contains the renal parenchyma that is divided into two parts, the cortex and the medulla. The medulla is the inner portion of the kidney which is approximately 5cm wide. It contains the loop of Henle, the vasa recta, the collecting ducts of the juxtamedullary nephrons while, the cortex which is approximately 1cm wide, is located farthest from the center of the kidney and around the outermost edges. It contains the nephrons (the structural and functional units of the kidney responsible for urine formation. The nephron is the microscopic structural. It is composed of a renal corpuscle and a renal tubule. The renal corpuscle consists of a tuft of capillaries called a glomerulus and an encompassing Bowman's capsule. The renal tubule extends from the capsule (Chalouhy, 2017; Wingerd & Taylor, 2020).

Furthermore, each kidney has one million nephrons that are located within the renal parenchyma and are responsible for the initial formation of urine. So, the large number of nephrons allows for adequate renal function even if, the opposite kidney is damaged or becomes nonfunctional but, if the total number of functioning nephrons is less than20 % of normal; renal replacement therapy needs to be considered (Wingerd & Taylor, 2020).

2-Anatomy of the Ureters, Bladder and Urethra

The urine formed in the nephrons flows through the renal pelvis and then into the ureters, which are long fibromuscular tubes that connect each kidney to the bladder; these narrow tubes, each 24 to 30 cm long, originate at the lower portion of renal pelvis and terminate in the trigone of the bladder wall. Where, the movement of urine from each renal pelvis through the ureter into the bladder is facilitated by peristaltic contraction of the smooth muscle in the ureter wall. In addition to, the urinary bladder is distensible muscular sac located behind pubic bone and the usual capacity of the adult bladder is 400 to 500 ml but, it can distend to hold a larger volume. Also, the urethra arises from the base of the bladder (Scanlon& Sanders, 2018) (Figure 2).

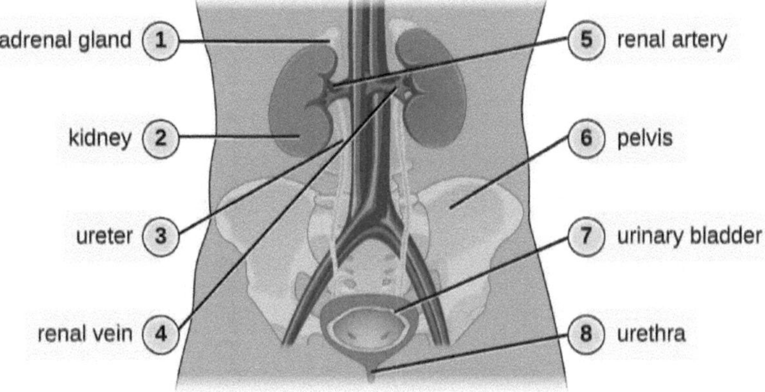

Figure2. Structures of the human urinary system are present in both males and females: *Delaney, Kowalewska, & Treuting, (2018). Urinary System in Comparative Anatomy and Histology (pp. 275-301). Academic Press, Available @https://www. google .com /search?q = structures of the human urinary system.*

Physiology of the Kidney

The kidneys maintain the body homeostasis including regulating acid base balance, the concentration of electrolytes, controlling blood pressure and secreting hormones, through removing and restoring selected amounts of solutes and water from the blood that, water balance is regulated by the kidneys and produces the formation of urine. Therefore, urine is formed in the nephron that, various substances excreted in the urine include sodium, chloride, bicarbonate, potassium, glucose, urea, creatinine and uric acid. Some of these substances are selectively reabsorbed into the blood. Also, the kidneys maintain the volume of electrolytes excreted per day which is equal to the amount ingested (Chalmers & Charlotte, 2019).

Regarding regulation of acid base balance, the kidneys have two major functions as follows: the first function is reabsorption bicarbonate from the urinary filtrate to the circulation of the body and the second function is excretion acid in urine. Also, the kidneys play a central role in the auto-regulation of arterial blood pressure where specialized vessels in the kidneys called vasa recta vessels that monitor blood pressure in the body once, detecting a decreased in blood pressure; specialized cells (denta cells) secrete the hormone renin (Scanlon & Sanders, 2018).

The hormone renin converts angiotensinogen which is produced in the liver to the hormone angiotensin1, then by angiotensin-converting enzyme found in lungs metabolizes angiotensin1 into angiotensin2 that causes blood vessels to constrict and the blood pressure to increase. Moreover, the hormone angiotensin 2 stimulates the adrenal glands to secrete hormone aldosterone which causes the renal tubules to retain sodium, water and excrete potassium. Together, angiotensin 2 and aldosterone work to raise blood volume, blood pressure and sodium levels in the blood to restore the balance of sodium and fluid. When the vessels recognize the increase in blood pressure; renin secretions stop by negative feedback mechanism that reduces output or activity to return an organ or system to its normal range of functioning (Fountain& Lappin, 2017).

Within the literature there are many other important kidney functions, as red blood cell production where, the kidneys detect a decrease in the oxygen concentration in renal blood flow, they release erythropoietin hormone (EPO) that stimulates the bone marrow to produce red blood cells which carry oxygen throughout the body (Gilan, Naseem, & Mohamed, 2018). Also, the kidneys have an important role in preventing all types of sleep disturbances (SD) as restless leg syndrome, sleep apnea, excessive day time sleepiness and insomnia (Maung et al., 2016).

Restless leg syndrome (RLS) is considered sensory motor disorder manifested by uncomfortable nocturnal sensation in the lower limb relieved by movement, caused by dropping in CSF ferritin levels through the night. Restless leg syndrome represents 3-7% in SD and 20-30% in ESRD. The Kidneys prevent restless leg syndrome, that it is responsible for secretion of EPO from the nephrons that stimulate bone marrow to secrete red blood cell, so prevent iron deficiency that brain iron plays important role in preventing RLS (Leschziner & Guy, 2018).

Sleep apnea is considered chronic disorder which causes repeated cessation of breath while patient is sleeping, caused by accumulation of fluid excess in the neck from the legs due to rostral shift that - fluid re-entering the venous system on lying down, leg blood volume decreases rapidly fluid distributed to the chest, neck and head with the effects of gravity - also, different positions overnight leading to upper airway restriction, collapse and higher rates of obstructive sleep apnea (OSA), it represents 2-4% in SD and 50-60%in the ESRD. Kidneys play important role in preventing sleep apnea by removing excess fluids from the body thus prevent rostral shift (Yayan, Rasche & Vlachou, 2017).

Excessive day time sleepiness is alert throughout the course of day, that caused by uremia and high prevelance of sleep apnea, it represents 10-12% in SD and 50% in the ESRD, so the main function of the kidney is excretion of waste products of metabolism in urine (Maung et al.,2016).

Insomnia is the inability to fall asleep or stay asleep and is characterized by poor sleep quality and poor quality of life. Also, there are many causes for insomnia, as older age, dialysis shift and melatonin hormone all play a role in the development of insomnia in patients undergoing hemodialysis. In addition to, insomnia represents 4-29% in SD and 50-75% in ESRD. So kidneys have very important role in preventing all types of SD. Moreover, the kidneys prevent dizziness by controlling blood pressure; prevent anemia and insomnia (Maung et al., 2016).

Overview of Renal Failure

Renal disease can get worse over time and may lead to renal failure. Renal failure (kidney failure), also known as End-Stage Renal Disease (ESRD) , is a medical condition in which the kidneys are functioning at less than 15% of normal. Renal failure is classified as acute renal failure, which develops rapidly and may resolve; and chronic renal failure, which develops slowly and can often be irreversible. Symptoms may include legs welling, feeling tired, vomiting, loss of appetite, and confusion. Complications of acute and chronic failure include uremia, high blood potassium, and volume overload. Complications of chronic failure also include heart disease, high blood pressure, and anemia (National Institute of Diabetes and Digestive and Kidney Diseases, 2017).

Pathophysiology of Renal Failure

The kidneys filter wastes and excess water from the blood in form of urine. When the kidneys can't remove the metabolic wastes of the body or perform their regulatory functions; the substances that, normally eliminated in the urine; accumulate in the body fluids as result of impaired renal excretion, fluid electrolyte and acid-base disturbance as well as affecting endocrine and metabolic functions. Renal failure is a systemic disease and a final common pathway of many different kidney and urinary tract diseases. Each year, the number of deaths from irreversible renal failure increases. There are many causes that impair renal function as hypovolemia, hypotension, reduce cardiac output and heart failure and obstruction of the kidney or lower urinary tract by tumor, blood clot or kidney stone. Theses causes lead to rapid loss of renal function causing acute renal failure (ARF) (Chen, Knicely & Grams, 2019).

Classification of Renal Failure

Acute Renal Failure

Acute renal failure is a rapid loss of renal function due to damage of the kidneys within hours; depending on the duration and severity of ARF. The causes of ARF are classified into pre renal, intrarenal and post renal failure. Pre renal failure, as

16

(hemorrhage, GIT losses, heart failure and sepsis); intra renal, as (ischemia, nephrotoxic agents and infectious disease); post renal failure, as (renal stone, tumors and strictures) (Makris & Spanou, 2016).

Acute renal failure is common and associated with serious short and long term complications. In addition to, the diagnosis of ARF is traditionally based on a rise in serum creatinine and fall in urine output. So, early diagnosis and identification of the underlying etiology are essential to guide management. In case of, Continuing ARF for more than 3 months leads to CRF (Ostermann & Joannidis, 2016).

Chronic Renal Failure

Chronic renal failure (CRF) is the 16th leading cause of death worldwide and is defined as a persistent abnormality in kidney structure or function (e.g. glomerular filtration rate GFR<60 ml/min/1.73 m^2) for more than 3 months. Chronic renal failure affects from 8% to 16% of the population worldwide (Chen et al., 2019). Furthermore, it considers as indicator of kidney damage and decreases renal function, also, it is associated with age-related renal function decline that, the patients incidence with CRF has increased particularly, when those patients have suffered from hypertension, diabetes, obesity and untreated or improperly treated ARF (Hill et al., 2016).

Patients with CRF have no or little symptoms till late in the stages, as frequent urination during the night may be the earliest symptom, decreased urination, swelling of legs, puffiness of face, shortness of breath, severe weight loss, ammonia breath, nausea and loss of appetite. Moreover, patients with CRF are complaining of many complications, such as uremia, anemia, peripheral neuropathy, osteopenia (reduction of bone tissue), fluid overload, congestive heart failure, hypertension, pericarditis, electrolyte imbalances and metabolic acidosis. Additionally, chronic renal failure has been classified into five stages, theses stages based on GFR that the normal GFR is $125ml/min/1.73m^2$ (Webster, Nagle, Morton & Masson, 2017).

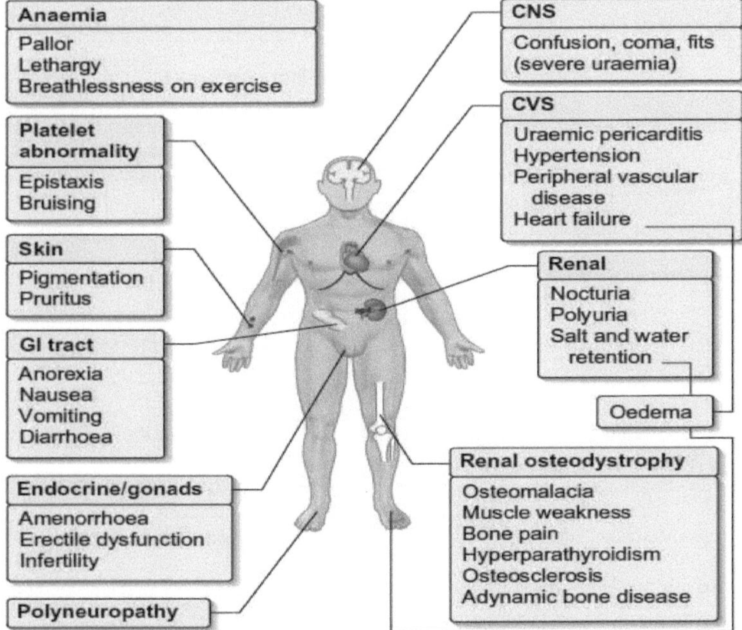

Figure3. Signs and symptoms of chronic kidney disease. *Fairweather, Findlay, & Isles, (2020). Overview of Chronic Kidney Disease, In Clinical Companion in Nephrology (pp. 119-124). Springer, Cham, Available@https://phacdochuabenh.com/Clinical-Medicine/ 88 .php.*

Stages of Chronic Kidney Disease

Stage1: Kidney damage with normal or increased GFR(≥90ml/min/1.73m2).

Stage 2: Mild decrease in GFR (60-89ml/min/1.73m2).

Stage 3: Moderate decrease in GFR (30-59ml/min/1.73m2).

Stage 4: Severe decrease in GFR (15-29 ml/min/1.73m2).

Stage5: End stage renal disease ESRD or chronic renal failure, GFR<15ml/min/

1.73 m2 (Doenges, Moorhouse & Murr, 2019).

Stage five ESRD occurs when the kidneys can't remove metabolic wastes of the body or perform their regulatory functions which is life threatening condition and is irreversible renal dysfunction that GFR<15 ml/min; so, those patients need regular interval of dialysis or renal transplantation to prevent serious complication and sustain life (Hill et al., 2016).

Management of Chronic Renal Failure

The goal of management is to maintain homeostasis of the body and is primarily with medications as (calcium and phosphate binders, antihypertensive agent and cardiovascular agents, antiseizure agents, erythropoietin) and diet therapy, although dialysis needed to decrease the level of uremic waste products in the blood and to control electrolyte balance. Selection of dialysis modality such as HD or PD depends largely upon physician recommendation, patient preference, and the patient's clinical and social status. Most of ESRD patients choose to be placed on lifelong HD machine to sustain life (Hill et al., 2016).

19

Overview of Hemodialysis

Hemodialysis treatment is a life-saving tool for those patients with ESRD by using machine to remove contaminated blood cleanses it and then returns it to the body through a filter, called a dialyzer (referred to artificial kidney) (Figure 4). Therefore, the blood is transported to and from the patient's body through a surgically created vein during this process such as Arteriovenous (AV) fistula, Arteriovenous (AV) graft or venous catheter (Mashkoor, 2016). Hemodialysis treatment is performed three times per week lasting three to four hours; the length of treatment depends on the amount of waste in body and the current state of health. Although hemodialysis is the most common methods to treat renal failure the patients undergoing HD still have wide range of problems and complications (Shim & Cho, 2017).

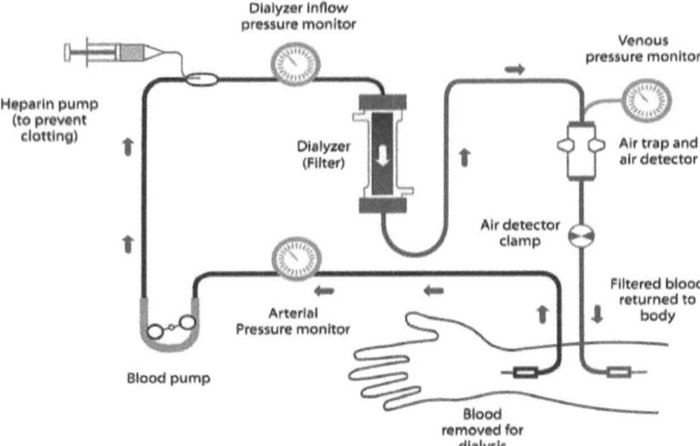

Figure4. Hemodialysis method. *Kallenbach, J. Z. (2020). Review of hemodialysis for nurses and dialysis personnel-e-book. Elsevier health sciences. Available @https://www. niddk.nih.gov/health-information/kidney-disease/kidney-failure/hemodialysis.*

Complications of Hemodialysis

The patients undergoing HD still have wide range of problems and complications such as muscle cramp, pruritus, abdominal pain, hypotension, hypertension, vomiting, short-term weight gain, constipation, chest pain, shortness of breath, dialysis disequilibrium, restlessness, air embolism if air enter the vascular system, nausea, anemia, headache, dizziness and sleeping disturbance (Pinheiro et al., 2017).The most widely reported symptoms are cramping (76%) headache (54%), pruritus (52%), back pain (51%), post dialysis dizziness (63%) and sleep disturbances (44%- 80%) (Fluck, 2016).

Sleep Disturbances

Normal Sleep

Sleep is a biologic process that is essential for life and optimal health. It is considered a basic state of rest and well-being for the mind and the body; sleep is a time of restoration and preparation for the next period of wakefulness (Koketus, 2017). Furthermore, it plays a critical role in brain function and systemic physiology: including metabolism, appetite regulation, supporting for the functioning of immune system, hormonal, cardiovascular system and the best way for coping with stress, solve problems and recover from illness (Tubbs, Dollish, Fernandez & Grandner, 2019).

Sleep releases human growth hormone for the repair and renewal of epithelial and specialized cells such as brain cells. Additionally, normal healthy sleep is characterized by sufficient duration, good quality, appropriate timing and regularity and absence of

21

sleep disturbances. It is also mentioned in the literature that, sleep is promoted by natural cycles of activity in the brain and consists of two basic states non-rapid eye movement(NREM)sleep and rapid eye movement (REM) sleep (Medic et al., 2017).

Sleep Cycle:

In the sleep cycle, there are two types of sleep; (NREM) sleep and (REM) sleep (Figure 5). Each sleep cycle occurs within 90 to 120 minutes; theses cycles are estimated to five sleep cycles a night for 7.5 hours of sleep. Usually, people begin the sleep cycle with a period of NREM sleep followed by a very short period of REM sleep (Tubbs et al., 2019).

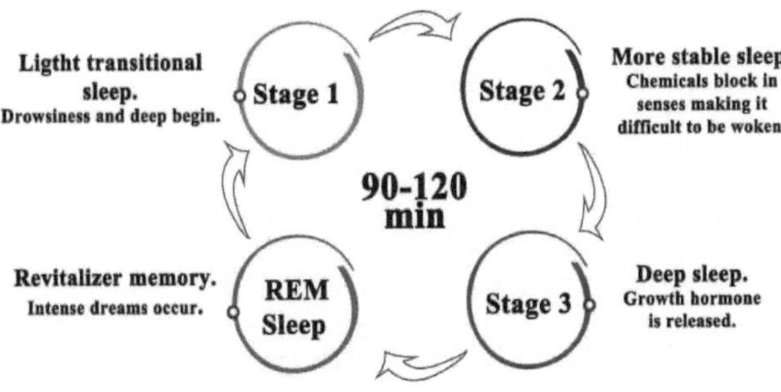

Figure5. Sleep cycle stages. *Chokroverty & Ferini-Strambi, (2017). Oxford textbook of sleep disorders. Oxford University Press. available @ https://www.aastweb.org/blog.*

Non-Rapid- Eye-Movements Sleep:

It is characterized by slow rolling eye movements and the absence of dreams. It represents about 80% of sleep with healthy adult sleep ranged from seven to eight hours a night. Also, this period is very important to the body that, the body repairs and regenerate tissues, builds bones and muscles and strengthens the immune system (Patel& Araujo, 2018). Additionally, there are many physiological changes that occur during NREM sleep, as slow and high-voltage of brain waves on the electroencephalographic (EEG), slow and regular of breathing and heart rate, low blood pressure and fragmented cognitive activity (Carley & Farabi, 2016). Moreover, NREM sleep involves light and deep sleep; firstly comes in sleep cycle followed by short period of REM sleep (Chokroverty & Ferini-Strambi, 2017).

NREM sleep is divided into four stages; each stage can last from 5 to 15 minutes or more; theses stages as follow: **Stage One**: This stage includes lightest level of sleep; this stage lasts 5 to 10 minutes. It is transition period between wakefulness and sleep also occurs between deep sleep (stage four) and REM sleep. It is characterized by decreased physiological activity begins with gradual fall in vital signs and metabolism, sensory stimuli such as noise and a person in this stage of NREM sleep can easily awoke (Sachdeva, 2019). **Stage Two**: This stage includes relaxation progresses, period of sound sleep, arousal is still relatively easy, lasts 10 – 20 minutes and body functions continue to slow (Sachdeva, 2019).

Stage Three: It is considered an initial stage of deep sleep that, it is difficult to arouse the sleeper and rarely moves, oxygen consumption, muscles are completely relaxed, vital signs decline but, remain regular and lasts 15–30 minutes. Also, this stage of NREM sleep assists the body to repair and regenerate tissue and the brain has the ability to flush out toxic waste (Brinkman & Sharma, 2019). **Stage Four**: It is the deepest stage of sleep; it is very difficult to arouse sleeper, vital signs are significantly lower than during waking hours, this stage lasts approximately15–30 minutes, Also, this stage of NREM sleep assists the body to repair and regenerate tissue, stimulates growth and development, boots immune function and builds up energy for the next day. Also, NREM sleep may repeat until REM sleep is attained (Dijket al., 2019).

Rapid-Eye-Movement Sleep:

It is a unique phase of sleep, characterized by random rapid movement of the eyes and accompanied by low muscle tone throughout the body and the tendency of the sleeper to dream clearly. Also, REM sleep comprises about 20-25% of total sleep in healthy adult sleep for seven to eight hours a night (Blumberg, Lesku, Libourel, Schmidt & Rattenborg, 2020). Additionally, this stage plays an important role in the regulation of emotions and linked these emotions to memories, decrease depression; anxiety; improve cognitive function and provide overall health benefits (Miller & Gehrman, 2019). Moreover, there are many physiological changes that occur during REM sleep, as low blood pressure, irregular fast breathing and heart rate, loss of skeletal muscle tone and gastric secretion increase (Jawabri, & Raja, 2020).

Physiological changes on body systems during the sleep:

Cardiovascular: Blood pressure decreases during NREM and REM sleep by about 10% and heart rate slows by 5% to 10%.The mechanism for this decline is caused by falling in sympathetic activity during sleep, which is responsible for the drop in blood pressure, cardiac output and systemic vascular resistance. This fall is accompanied by an increase in parasympathetic (vagal nerve) activity that is believed to be responsible for the bradycardia of sleep. Thus, the balance of parasympathetic/sympathetic activity is altered during NREM sleep, with the parasympathetic being dominant (Benarroch, E. E, 2019).

Respiratory: There is a decrease in respiratory rate and reduction in the muscle tone of the upper airway leading to decrease alveolar ventilation (Carley & Farabi, 2016).

Cerebral Blood Flow: NREM sleep is associated with significant reductions in blood flow and metabolism, while total blood flow and metabolism in REM sleep is comparable to wakefulness (Carley & Farabi, 2016).

Renal: There is a decreased excretion of sodium, potassium, chloride, and calcium during sleep that allows for more concentrated and reduced urine flow. Therefore, the changes that occur during sleep in renal function are complex and include changes in renal blood flow, glomerular filtration and hormones secretion (Chokroverty, Ferini-Strambi, 2017).

Endocrine: Endocrine functions such as growth hormone, thyroid hormone, and melatonin secretion are influenced by sleep whither, growth hormone secretion typically takes place during the first few hours after sleep onset while, thyroid hormone secretion takes place in the late evening (Chokroverty, Ferini-Strambi, 2017).

As far as importance of sleep on body systems there are many contributing factors causing sleep problems such as lifestyle and environmental factors, psychosocial issues and medical conditions. There are approximately 100 sleep disturbance classifications, however, they are usually manifested in one of the following three ways, as failure to obtain the necessary amount or quality of sleep (sleep deprivation), an inability to maintain sleep continuity - (disrupted sleep, also called sleep fragmentation, difficulty maintaining sleep and middle insomnia) -and events that occur during sleep (e.g., sleep apnea and restless legs syndrome) (Medic et al., 2017).

Sleep disorders

Sleep disorders are common in patients with end stage renal disease particularly on those undergoing dialysis therapies. It has been noted that 44%-80% of patients with end stage renal disease (ESRD) reported sleep complaints. Also, sleep disturbance in this population is associated with poor quality of life, depression, increasing systemic inflammation, cardio-vascular risk and mortality (Danielle et al., 2017). Additionally, many risk factors have been associated to sleep disturbance in patients with ESRD, such as older age, dialysis shift (morning or night), anemia, hypoalbuminemia, high parathyroid hormone (PTH) and chronic pain. Moreover, sleep disturbance includes a wide range of disorders such as insomnia, sleep-related breathing disorder and circadian rhythm sleep-wake disorder. Most of them have been described in patients undergoing hemodialysis, but sleep apnea, restless leg syndrome, excessive daytime somnolence and insomnia are mainly found (Danielle et al., 2017).

Insomnia

Insomnia is the most common sleep disorder affecting millions of people as either a primary or comorbid conditions - including patients on hemodialysis. It is defined as the subjective sensation of short and/or unsatisfying sleep or trouble falling asleep and/or to nighttime waking. In addition in most cases, the diagnosis of insomnia is based on the patient's history only; that commonly to accept these symptoms must be present at least three to four times a week for several weeks (Hamzi et al., 2017).

The etiology of insomnia is often multifactorial, as biochemical and metabolic changes, lifestyle factors, depression, anxiety, and other factors that affect the sleep and influence the efficacy of insomnia therapies. Examples of these factors include medical condition such as (obstructive sleep apnea, restless leg syndrome, mental health disorders and pain. Also complication of ESRD, such as (uremic toxin accumulation and inflammation), as well dialysis prescription aspects, such as modality, shift, and frequency of dialysis may affect sleep. Not only theses, but sleep hygiene as napping causing changes in sleep structure and circadian rhythm (Flythe et al., 2018).

Pathophysiology of Insomnia

There are alterations in circadian rhythm, sleep structure and alleviation of nocturnal melatonin surge among patients with ESRD. In a study of over 1600 patients on hemodialysis; 50% had trouble falling sleep, 50% woke up at night and 49% had early morning awakening over half reported one or more of these sleep-related symptoms all or most of the time. Moreover, insomnia is associated with worse quality of life and higher mortality among patients on hemodialysis (Flythe et al., 2018).

Insomnia may lead to long and short term consequences as follows: Long term consequences include hypertension that blood pressure (BP) varies over 24 hours. During normal sleep, BP typically decreases by 10% or more, starts to rise a few hours before waking up and continues to rise during the day, so insomniacs who sleep less than five hours a night are five times more likely to develop high BP (Thomas & Calhoun, 2017). Also, insomnia may cause cardiovascular disease that supposed mechanisms likely are due to increase activity of the sympathetic nervous systems, glucose metabolism alteration and possibly inflammation (Javaheri, & Redline, 2017).

Additionally, dyslipidemia may occur due to sleep fragmentation that can impair lipid metabolism (Lovato & Lack, 2019). Moreover, weight-related issues may take place as result of insomnia due to its effect on energy metabolism by two mechanisms; the first mechanism is impairing insulin sensitivity that is due to inability of glucose to mobilize itself independent of an insulin response or glucose doesn't respond to insulin response and the second one is increasing food intake so leading to weight gain (Medic et al., 2017).

Regarding to the short term consequences of insomnia, involve the impaired daytime functioning, increase stress responsivity that fragmented and interrupted sleep which lead to increase autonomic sympathetic activation Also, somatic pain may occur due to insomnia which is strongly associated with weekly headache and abdominal pain. Furthermore, the insomnia reduced quality of life, causes emotional distress, mood-cognitive-memory disorders and performance deficit. In addition, insomnia alters cognition and performance in many domains including attention, administrative function, emotional reactivity, memory formation, decision-making, risk-taking behavior, judgment, fatigue and dizziness (Medic et al., 2017).

Chronic pain; stress; older age; dialysis shift; melatonin all play a role in the development of insomnia among patients undergoing hemodialysis (Brown & Unruh 2020). Insomnia has a considerable impact on the quality of life of patients on dialysis. So it is essential to look for it and especially to determine the associated factors to be controlled (Arache, Laboudi, Ouanass & El Kabbaj 2019). In addition Lufiyani, Zahra, & Yona (2019) highlighted that the prevalence of insomnia tends to increase.

Pharmacological Treatment of Insomnia

The main goal of the treatment of insomnia is to improve subjective and objective sleep quality to eliminate or reduce insomnia and improve daytime functioning. So, pharmacologic treatment is mostly indicated for transient insomnia. There are many medications that used to treat the insomnia among patient undergoing HD. Although benzodiazepines are commonly used as hypnotics and have been shown to be effective in treating insomnia but, the medications have also been associated with a number of adverse effects as, dependence, abuse, potential impairment in daytime cognitive and psychomotor performance. Also, its adverse effects on respiration and the disruption of normal sleep architecture with a reduction in rapid eye movement (REM) (Maung et al., 2016).

Sedating antidepressants medication useful in the management of patients in whom depression and insomnia, but all antidepressants have potentially significant side effects such as dizziness, sedation and psychomotor impairment raise concerns about its use especially in the elderly (Wichniak, Wierzbicka, Walęcka & Jernajczyk, 2017). Antihistamines also used to treat insomnia and make patients feel sleepy, but increase risk of dementia. It is important to emphasize that, these drugs don't improve sleep and not helpful in the management of chronic insomnia (Grima, Bei & Mansfield, 2019).

Additionally, melatonin promotes sleep and is safe for short-term use. It is a natural hormone that plays a role in sleep wake cycle and synthesized mainly by the pineal gland located in the brain. So, it is recommended in patients with insomnia for regulation and improvement of the sleep-wake cycle with dose 3 mg of melatonin administered at bedtime respectively improved both subjective and objective sleep parameters, with no significant side effects reported as short-term use. Despite, continued used of melatonin is safe and well-tolerated option but, with long-term use doesn't sustain its efficacy at one year (Maung et al., 2016). Therefore, dialysis nurses have a primary role in conducting multidimensional assessments of patients, to understand the disease processes and ensure the co-morbidities and symptom burden from co-morbidities are adequately identified and managed. This requires a unique set of skills and expert knowledge to enable the delivery of person-centered care to patients with CRF (Chu, Szymanski, Tomlins, Yates & McDonald, 2018).

Nursing Management of Insomnia

Nursing management has a significant impact on the patient's recovery that nurse play significant role in management of insomnia among HD patients. Firstly through assessment, the nurse identifying changes that may lead to diagnosis of insomnia within patient's usual sleep habits, recent sleep quality as part of the initial nursing history. If sleep quality is reported to be poor, explore the nature of disturbance by noting the following: Assess severity of insomnia through observing and asking about difficulty falling asleep, difficulty staying a sleep problem, waking up too early besides, measure satisfaction of patient with sleep pattern and measure effect of insomnia on quality of life by using insomnia severity index tool (Lufiyani et al., 2019).

Additionally, it is important to assess nap time, number of sleep hours at night and any stressors that are impacting on the patient and consumption patterns like cigarette smoking before sleep hours. Furthermore, the nurse must assess and record all the prescribed and over counter drugs and supplements to determine if any of these substances has the potential to interfere with the patient's sleep. Moreover, reports by the sleep partner about any irregularities in terms of sleep such as snoring, periods of apnea, and restless leg movements which the patients most likely to be unaware of those problems (Lenggogeni, Sitorus& Maria, 2019).

Based on assessment data, the nurse should prepare educational intervention guidelines as Taha & Ali, (2015) developed guidelines to help improving patient's sleep through the following:

-Avoid caffeinated beverages and nicotine for at least six hours before bedtime and eating meals regularly and do not go to bed hungry or full stomach.

-Avoid naps if having trouble falling asleep at night and establish a regular routine for bedtime and morning awakening

-Use the bed only for sleep, but avoid reading or watching television and eliminate clocks in the bedroom.

-Use some maneuvers to reduce musculoskeletal tension before sleep, as calm breathing, relaxation exercises, and relaxation training.

-Increase knowledge of patient regarding his condition and related treatment; provide oral or written information as appropriate about, medication; follow up schedule; community resources and treatment options.

Also, Nursing interventions include education, training, behavioral, cognitive and dietary methods which help patients gain more knowledge of dialysis, in addition to, improve their compliance with this treatment (Hare, Clark-Carter, Forshaw,

2014). Besides, Nurses should take into consideration when caring for patients with insomnia the physical, psychological and social aspects of a patient's life, through providing optimal dialysis, a supportive environment, comprehensive-continuous education and ensuring holistic care (Taha & Ali, 2015).

Dizziness

Dizziness is a term used to describe a range of sensations, such as feeling light headed, faint, woozy, weak or unsteady and represents 63% of HD patients (Fluck, 2016; Kesser & Gleason, 2018).

Causes of dizziness

- **Sudden drop in blood pressure**. Low blood pressure occurs when too much fluid is removed from the blood during treatments which causes pressure to drop and dizziness as well as nausea and disequilibrium syndrome.

- **Decrease in blood volume**. A decrease in blood volume may cause inadequate blood flow to the brain. There are many Conditions such as cardiomyopathy, heart attack, heart arrhythmia and transient ischemic attack could cause dizziness

- **Medications.** Dizziness can be a side effect of certain medications - such as anti-seizure drugs, antidepressants and sedatives. In particular, blood pressure lowering medications may cause faintness

- **Anemia** (low iron). .Anemia causing fatigue, weakness and dizziness (Kesser & Gleason, 2018).

Regarding complication of dizziness, there are two term consequences a- short term consequences of dizziness may lead to increased risk of falling, injury and effect on daily life activities and b- long term outcomes as chronic dizziness (Sattar et al., 2016). And treated mainly through two prescribed medications, antihistamines and anticholinergic drugs but as any medication have many adverse effects that keep the nurse alert and provide essential nursing management for patients undergoing hemodialysis who are suffering from dizziness (Dyhrfjeld-Johnsen & Attali, 2019).

.**Nursing management of dizziness**

Dizziness can negatively affect the patient's life and cause injury. Since the cause of dizziness may be difficult to diagnose, nursing management should focus on the relieving dizziness. The main goal of nursing intervention Avoid complications of dizziness, decrease or prevent risk of injury, eliminate stress and anxiety, promote health status of patient and improve quality of life, Moreover, treatment strategies should include frequent monitoring to improve overall health or to deal with other conditions that may contribute to dizziness, safety measures to prevent falls, patient education about how to deal with dizziness (Gerretsenet al., 2019).

The nurse should take history of dizziness, identify causes of dizziness, determine onset, duration, number of episodes, triggers of dizziness and assess medication; some medication lead to dizziness such as antihypertensive agents, antianxiety agents and hypnotics. Also, assess the degree of anemia; vital signs especially blood pressure frequently. Also, it is essential to assess environment around the patient for factors known to increase fall risk such as unfamiliar setting and objects on the floor in addition to, assessment of the psychological problems such as fatigue, depression, sleep disturbance and dizziness among patients on HD (Pfieffer, Anthamatten & Glassford 2019).

Also assist and advice patient to change position slowly, teach patient avoid sudden position changes, avoid standing for short time, eat small meals frequently through the day to prevent low blood pressure and feeling dizziness, give cold compress and massage for head and neck to reduce feeling of lightheadedness and teach patient some relaxation technique (Park & Lee, 2019, Lam et al., 2019).

Additionally, elevate head of the bed as tolerated and encourage deep breathing exercises, teach patient to eat nutrient sources include iron, folic acid and vitamin B12 with amount according to doctor order, teach patient to monitor for hemoglobin level frequently and take appropriate medication for anemia that is one of the reasons of dizziness (Fraenkel, 2015).

Nursing Management of Patients Undergoing Hemodialysis

Nursing intervention has been progressively identified as being increasingly important to the improvement of patient's compliance with dialysis. Such interventions, including education, training and behavioral introduction, which help patients gain more knowledge of dialysis and develop healthy life habit (Wang et al., 2018).

Nephrology nurse play a vital role in the management of patients undergoing HD through checking the patient's vital signs and assess their condition, teaching patients about the disease, its treatment and answering any questions, overseeing the dialysis treatment from start to finish, making sure patients are given the correct prescribed medications, evaluating patient's reaction to the dialysis treatment and medications, reviewing the patient's lab work, home medications and activities and providing the physicians with information about changes in the patient's conditions (Ali, Salem& Salem, 2015).

Moreover, hemodialysis requires specialized nursing care that includes therapeutic and interpersonal relationships. In addition to providing high quality care to patients undergoing hemodialysis is a priority for nurses that nephrology nurses play a critical and valuable role in determining the efficiency and quality of care that patients receive. Since HD causes great amounts of fear and stress, patients on HD usually experience higher levels of psychosocial stress compared with levels of physiological stress due to low knowledge of self-care, poor performance in self-care and feeling of powerlessness. Nurse's knowledge about high-quality care and the means of providing it can increase patient satisfaction and improve patient-oriented care (Nobahar, 2017).

Hemodialysis nursing skills involve not only teamwork, but good assessment skills, technical skills, therapeutic communication, collaborative skills, documentation skills, good attention to detail and leadership qualities. There are many areas of knowledge that nephrology nurses provide to their patients other than just the technical aspects of dialysis care. Some of those may include the roles of caregiver, advocate, educator, facilitator, and mentor ((Richards, 2016; Wang et al., 2018).

In addition, teach patients how to manage their problems such as the maintenance of an acceptable blood pressure to control high blood pressure, restriction of fluid intake should be 500 ml to reduce salt and water retention, using antipruritic medications prescribed to reduce itching resulting from retention of urea and phosphate products. Encourage the patient to perform frequent mouth washes and taking small meals that are offered at a variety of intervals during the day to minimize anorexia (Terrill, 2016).

Hence, given the importance on the effect of insomnia and dizziness on body system, quality of life, daily functioning and the adverse effect of pharmacological treatments led to seeking complementary health approaches (CHAs) that concentrate on relaxation, reducing stress, help to calm emotions, relieve anxiety, increase general sense of health and well-being, improve sleep and relive symptoms of dizziness (Wagner, C. 2020; Yeung et al., 2018). The nurse should be aware and seek complementary health approaches (CHAs) to improve sleep and dizziness. Also, nurses promote complementary therapies as an opportunity to personalize care and practice in a humanistic way, obtain high quality of care for patients, reduce pharmacological therapy and its complications (Hall, Leach, Brosnan & Collins, 2017). It is mentioned in the literature that the most used therapies in CHAs are hydrotherapy, biofeedback, aromatherapy, relaxation technique, massage, acupuncture and acupressure therapy (Bossola et al., 2017)

Acupressure therapy

Acupressure therapy is the fifth most commonly used in CHAs and it was originated in ancient China and considered a treatment modality in Traditional Chinese Medicine (TCM) and a non-invasive variant of acupuncture form. Also, acupressure is a specific type of massage and showed superior therapeutic potential against numerous disease conditions. This technique was carried by applying pressure and massage of the thumbs or fingers and palms on specific points which are placed along the meridians to restore flow and balance to the physiological energy through the body and regulate opposing forces of negative and positive energy. Not only treats the energy fields and body, but also, the mind, emotions and spirit (Mehta et al., 2017).

It is highlighted in the literature that the meridians are the channels within human body which help to maintain energy and steadiness of health condition, each meridian is connected to various organs and tissues of human body. These energy meridians are essential to keep the body health, if this energy flow is blocked or not completely caused by stress, bad diet, drugs, injury and trauma…etc.; the body can no longer maintain the balance that is needed to maintain high energy and deal with health issues. Additionally, along the meridians lie acupressure points or acupoints, which may have therapeutic effect for certain medical condition when stimulated by pressure and massage (Waits, Tang, Cheng, Tai & Chien, 2018).

Acupoints are a cluster of pressure points within entire or whole human body. Acupoint is the point closest to the surface of the skin and activation of acupoint considers the prime or first step in acupressure procedure where there is area of high electrical conductance on the body surface. Also, stimulation of specified acupoints is known to elicit or arouse functional responses that can be used to treat many diseases. Moreover, application of pressure at different points causes different physical effect according to location (Wang & Hou, 2019).

Location of each acupoint on specified meridian is determined in terms of body inch or cun, inch /cun is known as Acupressure Units of Measurement (AUM). So, one inch/cun equals one thumb width at the base of the finger nail. As well acupoints can be activated by elbows, fingers, feet, palms, thumb or specific tools. Therefore, activation of specific point on these meridians by pressure and massage facilitates pain reduction, helps to relieve stress and tension, relaxes muscles and joints, improves sleep, minimizes headache; promotes blood circulation and strengthens immunity, in addition to treat the symptoms of dizziness (Figure 6). Also, acupressure is characterized by a manually operated, needle-free, non-invasive, cost-effective and non-pharmacological healing intervention to promote patient's well-being by acupressure stimulating the central nervous system and releasing chemicals into the muscles, spinal cord and brain. These biochemical changes may stimulate the body's natural healing abilities and promote physical and emotional well-being (Waits et al., 2018).

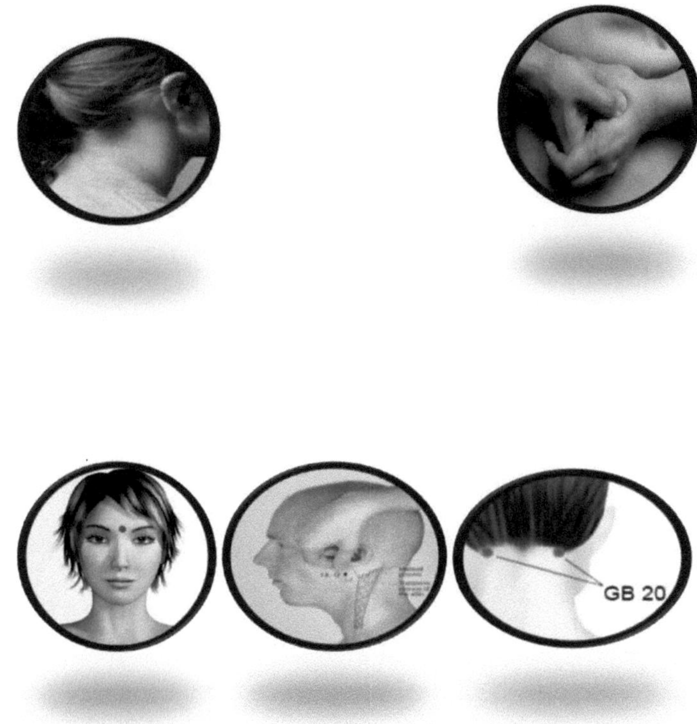

Figure6. Best Effective Acupressure Points for Sleeping Disorders (2017).
Available @https://acupressurepointsguide. com/acupressure-points-for-sleeping-
disorders/.

Biochemical mechanism of acupressure involves the stimulation of acupoints that leads to complex neuro-hormonal responses. Also, it modulates or adjusts the physiological response by increasing endorphin and serotonin transmittance to the brain and specific organs through nerves and meridians that provide relaxation for body and improve sleep and reduce symptoms of dizziness. Also it affects the level of stree hormone and lactic acid by restoring balance to the body and enable energy to circulate properly by unlocking the merdian pathways (Figure 6). This promotrs agreater sense of well-being by tacking the blockages stress causes (Mehta et al., 2017).

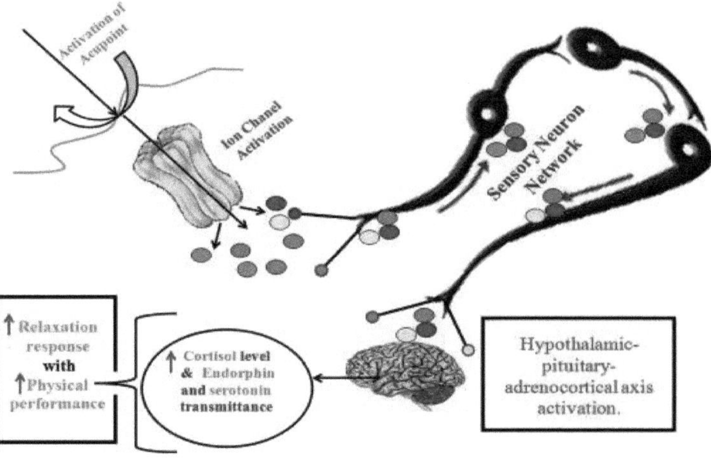

Figure7. Mechanism of acupressure. *Mehta, Dhapte, Kadam, & Dhapte (2017). Available @https://www.sciencedirect.com/.*

Meridian acupressure helps to change the concentration of stress hormones and lactic acid where acupressure activates myelinated neural fibers that stimulate the hypothalamus and pituitary gland leading to the release of β-endorphins from the hypothalamus into the spinal fluid and pituitary into the blood stream. Thus, the analgesic and sedative effect of β-endorphins facilitates rest and relaxation (Mehta et al., 2017). Given the importance of acupressure on the body, nephrology nurses should be aware of CHAs especially acupressure to control HD symptoms and treat insomnia and dizziness.

To sum up, patients on maintenance hemodialysis commonly complains of insomnia and dizziness. Poor sleep quality impairs their quality of life and adversely affects long-term outcomes. Acupressure therapy is a popular form of complementary medicine in China that treats various disorders by stimulating specific points. Learning acupressure technique as a non-pharmacological approach enriches nurses' knowledge and allows the nurse to gain the experience that can be brought to the clinical setting and by consequently optimizing quality of patient care.

Methods

Aim of the Study

The aim of the current study was to evaluate the effect of acupressure therapy on insomnia and dizziness among patients undergoing hemodialysis.

Research Hypotheses

To fulfill the aim of the study, the following research hypotheses were formulated:-

H_1: The study group patients who received acupressure therapy will have significant lower mean insomnia scores than control group who receive routine hospital care.

H_2. The study group patients who received acupressure therapy will have significant lower mean dizziness scores than control group who receive routine hospital care.

Research Design:

A quasi-experimental design (Time series design) was used in this study to estimate the causal impact of acupressure therapy(independent variable) on insomnia and dizziness level (dependent variable) on patients undergoing hemodialysis. This design lacks the element of random assignment but exercises certain controls of using some criterion other than random assignment such as eligibility and cutoff point. Also, time series design is created to strengthen quasi-experimental design. This design considers collection of observations sequentially through time (Chatfield, 2016).

Setting

The current study was carried out at Kasr EL-Aini Center (Nephrology-Dialysis – Transplantation) at Cairo University Hospital which consists of two sides with total capacity of 45 beds for HD patients. The first side consists of two rooms for hepatitis C virus (HCV) positive (containing eight HD machine) and one room for HCV negative (containing six HD machine) .The second side consists of seven rooms, two rooms for hepatitis C virus (HCV) positive (containing13 machine) and five rooms for HCV negative (containing18 HD machine) . The total number of patients divided in to two groups the first group come to the center on Saturday, Monday and Wednesday and another group come on Sunday, Tuesday and Thursday. Working system in the center is distributed in to two shifts per day on the first side and on the second side distributed in to three shifts. Total numbers of nurses in the center is 40 nurses.

Sample:

A nonprobability convenient consecutive sample of 88 adult male and female patients who have been on regular HD at least for 3 months and are able to communicate verbally constituted the study sample. The sample was equally divided into study and control groups. Patients with pacemaker, congestive heart failure, cancer, vestibular system disorders, or suffering from itching and redness on the prospect pressure points were excluded. The sample size calculated using a G-power version 3.1.1 (Cairo, Egypt) for power analysis. A power of 0.95 (β=1−0.95=0.05) at α 0.05 (one-sided tail) and the significance level of (P) less than or equal to 0.05 were utilized.

44

Tools of data collection:

To achieve the aim of the current study, three tools were utilized to collect data relevant to the study variables as follows:

Tool (1): Structured Interview Questionnaire: It was developed by the investigator; it includes two parts: **A**-Demographic data covering questions related to age, gender, level of education, occupation, marital status and residence. **B-** Medical related data such as current diagnosis, smoking history, current medication, associated diseases and lab investigation. **Tool (2):** Adopted Insomnia Severity Index (ISI) that was originally developed by Charles & Morin, 2003 The ISI consists of seven questions concerning sleep onset, sleep maintenance, early awakening, level of satisfaction with sleep pattern, extent of interference with daily functioning, result of impairment caused by sleep problems and level of concern about these problems. Each item is scored on a five-point Likert scale (zero to four). Total score ranged from 0 to 28. Scores zero to seven indicate no clinically significant insomnia, 8 to 14 sub-threshold insomnia (mild), 15 to 21 clinically significant insomnia (moderate), and 22 to 28 clinically significant insomnia (severe) with test- retest reliability of (r = 0.84). **Tool (3):** Dizziness Assessment Tool: This scale was developed by the investigator after extensive literature review to assess dizziness severity symptom and consists of 15 questions. Each item is scored on a ten-point Likert scale (zero to ten). Total score ranged from 0 to 150. Scores zero indicate no clinically significant dizziness, 1 to 50 sub- threshold dizziness (mild), 51 to 100 clinically significant dizziness (moderate) and 101 to 150 clinically significant dizziness (severe) with test-retest reliability of (r= 0.81).

Validity & Reliability of the tools

Content validity of the study tools was reviewed by a panel of five experts in Medical Surgical Nursing department from Faculty of Nursing and physiotherapist from dialysis unit, Cairo University. The experts were asked to examine the instruments for content coverage, clarity, wording, length, format, and overall appearance. On the other hand reliability of the tool three was tested using test – retest reliability.

Pilot Study

A pilot study was conducted on 10% of the sample to ensure objectivity, feasibility of the study as well as to examine issues related to the design, sample size, time required for data collection, procedures and data analysis approaches.

Ethical Consideration

The approval to conduct the proposed study was obtained from the Research and Ethics Committees at Faculty of Nursing, Cairo University (IRB 00004025). Also an official permission was obtained from hospital/clinic administrators where the study was conducted. Each patient was informed about the nature and purpose of the study as well as risks and benefits involved. The investigator emphasized that participation in the study is voluntary. Participants can withdraw from the study at any time without effect on the medical care they receive. Then, those who choose to participate in the study were asked to sign the consent form. Additionally, confidentiality and anonymity was assured through coding the data.

Procedure

The current study was conducted through the following dynamic three phases: Preparatory, Implementation and Evaluation. **Preparatory Phase**: This phase includes thorough review of literature related to managing patients on hemodialysis as well as the uses of non-pharmacological therapy with a focus on acupressure. In addition to, searching for the availability of the tools, during this phase the investigator developed Dizziness Assessment Tool and all necessary steps for nursing instruction booklet preparation were carried out. This phase took nearly four and half months. Furthermore, during this phase the investigator attended acupressure therapy course for three months in Acupressure Therapy Center in Egypt. **The implementation phase**: Once official permission is granted to proceed with the proposed study. The investigator initiated collecting demographic and medical related data using tool (1) which was followed by filling out tools number (2 & 3) to assess initial level of insomnia and dizziness among the patients under the study. Then, in brief the investigator explained individually the content of the booklet to the participants in the study group to ensure their full cooperation.

After that, the investigator began to apply acupressure technique to the study group participants at the rate of three sessions per week for one full month for each patient in the study group according to Traditional Chinese Medicine Protocol (TCM) on eight points at the right and left side of the body which are: Yintang (EX 2), Yifeng (SJ17 sanyinjiao), Anmian (EX22), Fengchi (GB20), Hegu (LI4). The pressure for each point took one minute divided as follows: 30 seconds for pressure, 14 seconds to apply circular motion clockwise, 14 seconds counterclockwise and two seconds for rest for this point; the time was calculated using stop watch. This technique was repeated for three times for each point, therefore, the total time of pressure for each point was three minutes and the total time for each patient was 24 minutes. In relation to the control group, they were receiving routine hospital care in this period. **Evaluation phase:** During this phase two follow up assessments were done for both groups upon completion of 6 and 12 sessions from initial assessment respectively. These two assessments were done through filling Insomnia Severity Index (ISI tool 2) and Dizziness Assessment Tool (tool 3). This phase took nearly six months. To apply the principle of fairness, the booklet was explained for the participants in the control group by the investigator upon completion of the study.

Statistical Design

Obtained data was tabulated, computed and analyzed using Statistical Package for the Social Sciences (SPSSx) version 23. Descriptive statistics such as frequency, percentage, mean and standard deviation, in addition to, inferential statistics including Paired T-test, Anova, and Chi-square test were utilized to analyze data pertinent to the study variables of insomnia and dizziness. Level of probability errors were adopted at $P \leq$ 0.05.

48

Results

Insomnia and dizziness are the most common problems among patients undergoing HD. Acupressure is a specific type of massage and showed superior therapeutic potential against numerous symptoms such as insomnia and dizziness (Mehta et al., 2017).The aim of this study was to evaluate the effect of acupressure therapy on insomnia and dizziness among patients undergoing hemodialysis. The total number of the studied subjects was 88 adult male and female patients at least 3 months on regular hemodialysis and admitted to Nephrology-Dialysis-Transplantation Center at Kasr EL-Aini Hospital-affiliated to Cairo University Hospital.

To fulfill the aim of this study, the following research hypotheses were formulated.

H_1: The study group patients who received acupressure therapy will have significant lower mean insomnia scores than control group who receive routine hospital care.

H_2. The study group patients who received acupressure therapy will have significant lower mean dizziness scores than control group who receive routine hospital care.

Statistical findings of the current study were presented in the following order: **Section (I):** Devoted to describe the demographic characteristics and medical related data (Tables 1- 4). **Section II**: Represented statistical analysis for study hypotheses among the study and control groups (Tables 5-6 &Figures 8-9). While, **Section III**: Illustrated additional and correlation findings between insomnia and dizziness by using Paired T-test, Anova and Pearson correlation coefficient (table 7-9 &Figure 10).

Section (I): Describes the demographic characteristics and medical related data among the study and control groups.

Table 1

Frequency and percentage distribution of demographic data among the study and control groups (N =88) (44/each).

Variables	Study group		Control group		Chi-square	*P – value
	No.	%	No.	%		
Age						
20-<40	15	34	13	29.5	0.23	0.88
40-<60	20	45.5	22	50.0		
≥60	9	20.5	9	20.5		
Mean±SD	47.3±14.5		48.2±14.0			
Gender						
Male	12	27.3	25	56.8	7.88	0.004*
Female	32	72.7	19	43.2		
Job/Occupation						
No work	38	86.4	39	88.6		
Working	6	13.6	5	11.4	1.04	0.59
Level of education						
Can't read or write	11	25.0	10	22.7	4.2	0.52
Read and write	0	0	3	6.8		
Primary	10	22.7	8	18.2		
Preparatory	4	9.2	4	9.1		
Secondary	13	29.5	10	22.7		
College	6	13.6	9	20.5		
Residence						
Rural	4	9.1	4	9.1	00	1.0
Urban	40	90.9	40	90.9		
Marital status						
Single	9	20.5	4	9.1	7.37	0.06
Married	23	52.2	34	77.3		
Widow	7	15.9	2	4.5		
Divorced	5	11.4	4	9.1		

*Significant at $P \leq 0.05$

Table (1) revealed that, the mean age ±SD of the study and control group were 47.3 ±14.5 and 48.2±14.0 years respectively.   72.7% of the study group was female compared to 43.2% of the control group with χ^2 = 7.88 and P value = 0.004. The similarity of occupation among subjects in both groups is apparent; as 86.4% of the study group and 88.6% of the control group were not working. Concerning the level of education 29.5% of study group and 22.7% of control group had secondary education level. This table also, illustrated that 90.9% of both groups were from urban areas. In addition, 52.2% and 77.3% of the study and control groups respectively were married.

Table 2

Frequency and percentage distribution of medical related data among the study and control groups (N =88) (44/each).

Variables	Study group		Control group		Chi-square	*P-value
	No.	%	No.	%		
Chronic Associated diseases						
Yes	34	77.3	31	70.5	7.1	0.31
No	10	22.7	13	29.5	0.52	0.46
*Among yes						
Diabetes	6	17.6	4	12.9	`	
Hypertension	18	52.9	19	61.3		
Diabetes and hypertension	5	14.7	3	6.7		
Others	12	35.3	8	25.8		
Smoking						
Yes	5	11.4	8	18.2	15.21	0.76
No	39	88.6	36	81.8	0.81	0.36
Hours of sleep at night					0.09	0.95
4	2	4.5	2	4.5		
6	35	79.5	36	81.8		
8	7	16.0	6	13.7		
Nap time /day					3.78	0.052
Yes	13	29.5	5	11.4		
No	31	70.5	39	88.6		

*Significant at $P \leq 0.05$

*Not mutually exclusive, Patient suffers from more than one disease.

Table (2) clarified that, 77.3% of the study group and 70.5% of the control group were suffering from different chronic associated diseases especially hypertension which represent 52.9% and 61.3% respectively. In relation to the numbers of sleep hours at night 79.5% and 81.8% of the study and control groups respectively reported that, they sleep six hours/night and suffering from interrupted sleep. In addition, 70.5% and 88.6%

of the study and control groups respectively did not take nap time with χ^2 =3.78 and P value = 0.052.

Table 3

Frequency and percentage distribution of current medication among the study and control groups on (N =88) (44/each).

Medication / dose	Study group		Control group		Chi-square	*P-value
	No.	%	No.	%		
					2.48	0.11
Norvasc 5 mg	29	65.9	13	29.5		
Folic acid 5 mg	23	52.3	9	20.5		
Eprex 4000 units	23	52.3	35	79.5		
Capotin 5 mg	2	4.5	00	00		
Calcimate 500 mg	36	81.8	18	40.9		
Vit. B complex amp(2ml)	27	61.4	35	79.5		
Renagel 800 mg	13	29.5	9	20.5		
Carnitine amp (1g)	6	13.6	9	20.5		
Zantac 150 mg	4	9.1	00	00		

*Significant at $P \leq 0.05$
*Not mutually exclusive, Patient takes more than one medication.

As seen in table (3), there was no significant difference between the study and control group in relation to medications administration and its doses (χ^2 = 2.48, P= 0.11) as 81.8%, 65.9%, 61.4% and 52.3% of study group receiving Calcimate, Norvasc, Vit B complex, folic acid and Eprex 4000 units respectively. While, 40.9 %, 29.5%, 20.5% and 79.5% of the control group receiving Calcimate, Norvasc, folic acid, Vit B complex and Eprex 4000 units respectively.

53

Table 4

Mean values of Lab investigation among the study and control groups (N=88) (44/each).

Lab investigation	Study group mean value	Control group mean value	t-value	*P-value
Calcium	7.2	6.3	2.99	0.004*
Hemoglobin	9.4	9.8	1.37	0.17
Phosphate	7.3	7.1	0.66	0.51
Urea	121	105	4.28	0.0001*

*Significant at $P \leq 0.05$

Table (4): Summarized that there was highly significant difference between both groups in relation to the calcium level (t = 2.99, P = 0.004*) and urea level (t = 4.28, P = 0.0001*). While, there was no significant difference between both groups in relation to the hemoglobin level (t = 1.37, P = 0.17) and phosphate level (t = 0.66, P = 0.51).

Section II: Represents statistical analysis for the study hypotheses among the study and control groups.

Table 5

Frequency and percentage distribution of insomnia levels among the study and control groups at baseline, after 6 sessions, and after 12 sessions (N=88) (44/each).

Insomnia Levels	Baseline				After 6 sessions				After 12 sessions			
	Study		Control		Study		Control		Study		Control	
	No.	%	No.	%	No.	%	No.	%	No.	%	No.	%
None	4	9.1	2	4.5	12	27.3	5	11.4	13	29.6	6	13.6
Mild	12	27.3	16	36.4	13	29.5	13	29.5	13	29.5	12	27.3
Moderate	23	52.3	22	50.0	18	40.9	22	50.0	18	40.9	22	50.0
Severe	5	11.4	4	9.1	1	2.3	4	9.1	00	0.0	4	9.1
χ^2	1.37				5.08				28.7			
***P-value**	0.71				0.16				0.0001*			

*Significant at $P \leq 0.05$

As regards insomnia level, table (5) illustrated that, there was highly significant difference between study and control groups in relation to insomnia level after 12 sessions ($\chi^2 = 28.7$, P = 0.0001*). Therefore, the first hypothesis of the current study was supported.

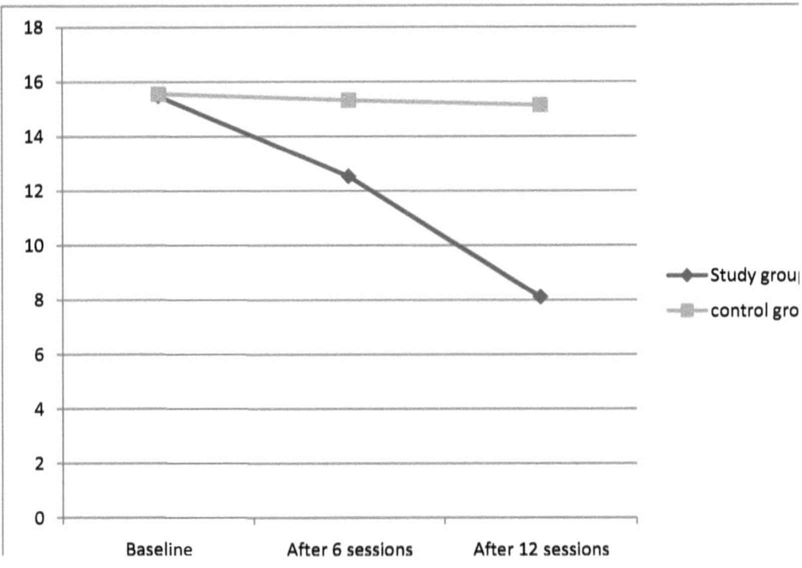

Figure8. Difference between insomnia levels in both groups on each time at baseline, after 6 sessions, and after 12 sessions (N=88) (44/each).

Figure (8) clarified a meaningful reduction in the insomnia level among the study group; as insomnia mean score decreased from 16 at baseline to 12 after 6 sessions to 8 after 12 sessions. While in the control group remained nearly the same at the three times; which indicate the difference between the study and control group.

Table 6

Frequency and percentage distribution of dizziness levels among the study and control groups at baseline, after 6 sessions and after 12 sessions (N=88) (44/each).

Dizziness Levels	Baseline				After 6 sessions				After 12 sessions			
	Study		Control		Study		Control		Study		Control	
	No.	%	No.	%	No.	%	No.	%	No.	%	No.	%
None	0	0	0	0	0	0	0	0	1	2.3	0	0
Mild	37	84.1	37	84.1	42	95.5	38	86.4	43	97.7	38	86.4
Moderate	7	15.9	7	15.9	2	4.5	06	13.6	0	0	6	13.6
Severe	0	0	0	0	0	0	0	0	0	0	0	0
χ^2	00				2.2				7.3			
*P-value	1.0				0.13				0.02*			

*Significant at $P \leq 0.05$

Concerning dizziness level, table (6) refined that, there was a significant difference between the study and control groups in relation to dizziness level after 12 sessions (χ^2 = 7.3 and P = 0.02*). Therefore, the second hypothesis of the current study was supported.

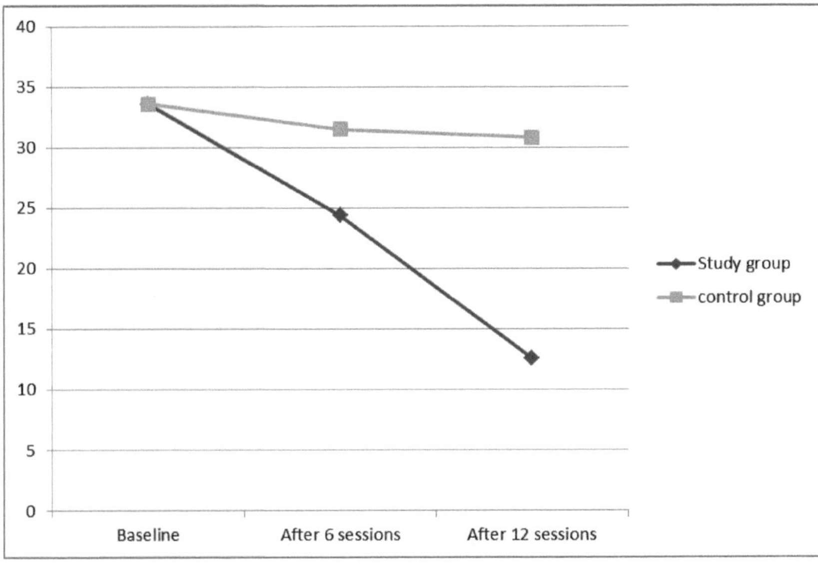

Figure9. Difference between dizziness levels in both groups on each time at baseline, after 6 sessions, and after 12 sessions (N=88) (44/each).

Figure (9) illustrated a noticeable reduction in the dizziness level in the study group as dizziness mean score decreased from 35 at baseline to 25 after 6 sessions to 12 after 12 sessions. While in the control group remained nearly the same at the three times; which indicate the difference between the study and control group.

Section III: Illustrates additional and correlation findings between insomnia and dizziness by using Paired T-test, Anova and Pearson correlation coefficient

Table 7

Comparison of mean scores related to different insomnia and dizziness assessments among the study and control groups (N=88) (44/ each).

Scale	Study group			Control group		
	Baseline and First assessment	Baseline and Second assessment	First and Second assessment	Baseline and First assessment	Baseline and Second assessment	First and Second assessment
	Paired T-test Result					
Insomnia	8.12	23.7	16.7	1.9	2.3	1.7
*P value	0.0001**	0.0001**	0.0001**	0.06	0.02*	0.08
Anova	2.74 P=0.008*			0.0 P=0.9		
Dizziness	**Paired T-test Result**					
	9.6	18.4	12.9	1.3	1.3	1.3
*P value	0.0001**	0.0001**	0.0001**	0.18	0.18	0.18
Anova	1.45 P=0.18			0.0 P= 0.7		

*Significant at $P \leq 0.05$

Table (7) clarified that, there was highly significant difference between baseline and first assessment, baseline and second assessment, first and second assessment mean scores regarding insomnia levels as follows t = 8.12; 23.7; 16.7 respectively at (P =0.0001) among the study group with ANOVA = 2.74 at (P = 0.008). While there was a significance difference only between baseline and second assessment mean scores among the control group as t=2.3, at (P =0.02), ANOVA at (P = 0.9). In reference to dizziness levels, the table disclosed that, there was highly significance difference between baseline and first assessment, baseline and second assessment and first and second assessment mean score as t = 9.6; 18.4; 12.9 at (P =0.0001) among the study group with ANOVA = 1.45 at (P = 0.18). While there was no significance difference between the three different assessments mean scores among the control group as t=1.3 at (P =0.18) with ANOVA at (P = 0.7).

Table 8

Correlation between insomnia and dizziness among the study and control groups using Pearson Correlation Coefficient (N=88, 44/ each).

Variables	Insomnia			
	Study		Control	
	r	P	r	P
Dizziness	0.55	0.0001*	0.56	0.0001*

*Significant at $P \leq 0.05$

It is clear from table (8) that, there was strong positive correlation between insomnia and dizziness levels among the study and control groups which indicates the reciprocal relation between insomnia and dizziness levels (r = 0.55, P = 0.0001* and r = 0.56, P = 0.0001*) respectively.

Table (9)

Correlation between age and insomnia and dizziness among the study and control groups (N=88) (44/ each).

Variables	Age	
	R	P
Insomnia	0.11	0.21
Dizziness	0.004	0.96

*Significant at $P < 0.05$

Table (9) clarified that, there was no correlation between insomnia and dizziness levels with age among the study and control group subjects' (r = 0.11, P = 0.21 and r = 0.004, P = 0.96) respectively.

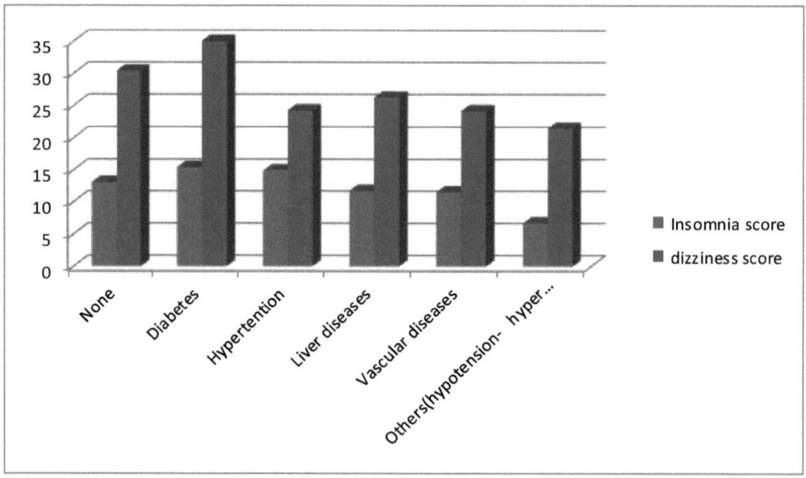

Figure10. Correlation between associated diseases with insomnia and dizziness among the study and control groups (N=88) (44/ each).

Figure (10) indicated that, there was no correlation between associated diseases with insomnia and dizziness among the study and control group' (ANOVA= 1.83, P = 0.1 and ANOVA = 0.98, P = 0.43) respectively.

Discussion

Insomnia and dizziness are among the most important health problems worldwide facing patients on hemodialysis with significance physical, psychological and economic impact. On the other hand, acupressure is one of the non-pharmacological therapies used to improve patient sleep and decrease dizziness symptoms for patients on hemodialysis (Shim & Cho, 2017). A discussion of the findings is presented in the following sections (a) Demographic and medical background information, (b) the effectiveness of acupressure on insomnia and dizziness level as stated in the current study hypotheses, and (c) the relationship between selected patients' demographic variables and both insomnia and dizziness levels.

Section I: Demographic and medical background information

The current study findings revealed that, approximately half of study and control group their age ranged between forty to less than sixty with a mean of age 47.3 ± 14.5 and 48.2±14.0 respectively; which clarified the homogeneity of the studied subjects. This finding is consistent with Hamzi et al., (2017) as they conducted a study related to "Insomnia in hemodialysis patients" on 125 patients and found that, the studied subjects mean age was 54.3±13.2 years. Additionally, a study carried out by Alkhuwaiter, Alsudais & Ismail, (2020) entitled "A prospective study on prevalence and causes of insomnia among end-stage renal failure patients on hemodialysis in selected dialysis centers in Qassim, Saudi Arabia", as the researchers found that, median age of the studied subjects was 60.

However, another study carried out by Allah, Abdel-Aziz & El-Seoud, 2014 on 107 patients observed that the mean age among the studied subjects was 66.8±5.0 years. Also, another study conducted by Ahmed et al., (2017) entitled that "The effects of age and gender on the prevalence of insomnia in a sample of the Saudi population", as they found that 93.7% of their participants age among elderly group was higher than the middle and young aged. the age differences between these researchers could be explained in the light of CDC, (2019) report which stated that chronic renal failure can develop at any age but become more common with increasing age as after the age 40. Additionally, kidney filtration begins to fall by approximately 1% per year (Allah et al., 2014).

Regarding gender, the current study findings revealed that, there was a statistically significant differences between the study and control groups as more than two third of the study group were female in comparison to more than half of the control group were male. This finding is consistent with Hamzi et al., (2017); Bhaskar, Hemavathy & Prasad, (2016) that the researchers found that more than half of the studied subjects were female. Furthermore, Alkhuwaiter et al., (2020) documented that 56% from studied sample was female.

Moreover, this finding is incongruent with a study carried by Leschziner, (2018) titled "Restless-legs syndrome in Dialysis Patients" clarified that, more than half of the study sample was male. Instead Arache et al., (2019), who assess poor quality of sleep in

52 patients on hemodialysis, reported that the male: female ratio was 1.1.While, CDC, (2019) clarified that CRF is more common in women (15%) than men (12%).

Also, John, Mboto & Agbo, (2016) who conducted a study in Nigeria entitled "A review on the prevalence and predisposing factors responsible for urinary tract infection among adults" and at the same line with the current study findings explained that Chronic kidney disease (CKD) is common among the elderly people with increased rate of infections among which UTI is most. The prevalence of urinary tract infection is high in females compared to the males this could be due to anatomical structure of female body as the female urethra appears to be particularly prone to colonization because of its proximity to the anus. From the investigator' opinion the sampling technique utilized in this study may explain this differences.

In relation to marital status; the current study displayed that, the most of the studied subjects was married which is expected among this age group in Egyptian culture. This finding is supported by Kumar & Sagar, (2019) who reported that, the majority of their studied subjects were married likewise, Mahmoud, AboZead, Mohammad, El-all & ElRazik, (2019) documented the same finding.

Concerning educational level, the current study documented that, near to one third of the participants fall into the literate category (secondary education). This finding is in agreement with Kumar & Sagar, (2019) in India, who documented that more than half of their studied subjects were literate. Also, Mahmoud et al., (2019) in Egypt mentioned that, the majority of their studied subjects were literate. Nevertheless, the finding is inconsistent with a study carried by NoroziFiroz, Shafipour, Jafari, Hosseini, &Yazdani-Charati, (2019) in Iran, who observed that around half of their studied subjects were illiterate. This discrepancy could be interpreted by the facts that, the majority of the subjects in the current study were from urban areas and people living in this area are interested in education.

The current study findings showed that, the majority of the studied subjects were had no work. This finding is consistent with Bhaskar et al., (2016) in a study entitled "Prevalence of chronic insomnia in adult patients and its correlation with medical co-morbidities" and the researchers reported that, more than one third of the studied subjects were unemployed unlike conducted study by Mahmoud et al., (2019) reported that the majority of their studied subjects were unemployed. The rational of unemployment explained in the light of the predominant symptoms of hemodialysis which affect negatively person's ability to work as well as the duration and the repetition of hemodialysis sessions. The investigators opinion in relation to this point is that subjects undergoing HD spent four hours for three times per week, therefore, no institution accepts interrupted working hours.

In reference to place of residence, the current study illustrated that, the majority of the studied subjects were from urban areas. This finding matched with Allah et al., (2014) who conducted a study in Zagazig City, Egypt. This finding could be explained by the fact that, the great majority of Egyptians-estimated 80 million people live near the banks of the Nile River, where arable land is found. Another possible explanation that might partially account for this finding is the prevalence of chronic glomerulonephritis; renal calculi; schistosomiasis that are positively associated with the onset CRF (Ghonemy, Farag, Soliman, El-Okely& El-Hendy, 2016).

Yet, the current finding is incongruent with study conducted in India by Aggarwal, Jain, Dabas & Yadav, (2017); also, Mahmoud et al., (2019) in Assiut University, Egypt, as they reported that, the majority of their studied subjects were from rural areas; geographical distribution of the population in different countries might account for the differences in the study findings. Also, in urban areas most of the people working at industries and people exposed to radiate substances that lead to renal disease such as lead, chromium and mercury. In addition to atmospheric environment in urban areas, as an environmental factor the incidence of pollution from cars and industries may be lead to kidney disease.

The current study reported that, almost half of the studied subjects in the study and control group had hypertension (HTN) and followed by diabetes mellitus (DM). Similar findings concerning hypertension were also expressed by Yildiz et al., (2016), as HTN represented around one third of their studied subjects and Allah et al., (2014), also reported that less than half of studied subjects were suffering from HTN. Also, Kumar & Sagar, 2019 reported that higher percentage of their studied subjects had hypertension. Another study conducted by Bhaskar et al., (2016) indicated that higher percentage of the studied subjects had diabetes. Also, DM was reported by half of the patients in a study conducted by Alkhuwaiter et al., (2020). These returns could be interpreted by the fact that, diabetes and hypertension are significantly associated with the impairment of renal function, particularly among younger age with hypertension (Yuejuan et al., 2017).

It was observed from the findings of the current study that two third of the studied subjects were not smoker, this finding was in the same line with Mahmoud et al., (2019) who conducted a study entitled "Assessment Quality of Sleep in Patients undergoing Hemodialysis" they reported that, majority of the studied subjects were not smoking. Likewise, a study by Allemand, Nóbrega, Lauar, Veiga & Camargos, (2017) entitled "Sleep Parameters in Short Daily versus Conventional Dialysis: An Actigraphic Study" reported that more than three quarters of their studied subjects were not smoking. Another study conducted by NoroziFiroz et al., (2019) entitled " Relationship of Hemodialysis Shift with Sleep Quality and Depression in Hemodialysis Patients", and the researchers reported that one third of their studied subjects were smoker.

Concerning the numbers of hours of sleep at night, the current study documented that the majority of the studied subjects were complaining from interrupted sleep hours at night. This finding matched with Hamzi et al., (2017), as they reported that the majority of study subjects complained of interrupted sleep. Also, Wang et al., 2016, as carried out a study entitled "Poor sleep and reduced quality of life were associated with symptom distress in patients receiving maintenance hemodialysis" and reported that the majority of their studied subjects complained of interrupted sleep hours.

In relation to receiving medications, it was observed in the current study that patients undergoing hemodialysis receiving two types of antihypertensive medications; The number of antihypertensive drugs used increased as patients neared ESRD, this finding matched with study conducted by Chang, Zheng, Montez-Rath & Winkelmayer, (2016) entitled "Antihypertensive medication use in older patients transitioning from chronic kidney disease to end-stage renal disease on dialysis", and reported that multidrug antihypertensive therapy was common among patients undergoing HD and was associated with significant decrease in BP. Also, added that antihypertensive drugs were prescribed for the majority of the patients and around quarter required two or more drugs.

Moreover, anemia is a frequent complication of chronic renal failure, so patients undergoing HD in the current study are receiving anemic medications to avoid complication of anemia and reduce the need for blood transfusions but not to increase hemoglobin level. Similar study concerning anemia was also expressed by Hasegawa, Koiwa & Akizawa, (2018), entitled " Anemia in conventional hemodialysis: Finding the optimal treatment balance", as the researchers expressed that an effective use of iron preparations is required to yield the optimal effect of erythropoiesis-stimulating agents (ESAs). It is well-known that iron utilization is inhibited under pathological conditions (Michał et al., 2020).

Also, the current study finding is similar to study conducted by Ibrahim et al., (2018), as they conducted a study entitled "Medication discrepancies in late-stage chronic kidney disease" and reported that all patients with late stage-chronic renal failure receiving more than one medications, these medications include cardiovascular, vitamins, mineral disease agents, anemia and GIT problems medications.

In relation to laboratory investigation; the current study evidenced that, all study participants have low hemoglobin levels, this finding is in the same line with a study conducted by NoroziFiroz et al., (2019) entitled "Relationship of Hemodialysis Shift with Sleep Quality and Depression in Hemodialysis Patients" and reported that more than half of their studied subjects had low hemoglobin level.

Also, the current study documented that all studied subjects have low calcium levels, The explanation to this finding that decreasing awareness of patients undergoing HD about foods that naturally contain calcium and not separating with diet containing calcium and phosphorus as spinach and sardines that may not be recommended for the CRF diet. This finding matched with study of Thongprayoon et al., (2018) entitled "Hypocalcemia and bone mineral density changes following denosumab treatment in end-stage renal disease patients: a meta-analysis of observational studies", and reported that one third of studied subjects had low calcium levels. This could be due to hypocalcaemia in chronic renal failure is caused by two primary factors - increased serum phosphorus and decreased renal production of vitamin D (Goyal & Singh, 2020).

Also, the current study findings showed that, more than half of the studied subjects have high phosphate levels. This explanation is due to decreasing knowledge and awareness of patients undergoing HD about diet that contain phosphate. In addition to, high phosphate level is considered as a complication of CFR and decrease calcium level. This finding matched with Rabbani & Rao, (2017) who conducted a study titled " Hyperphosphatemia in end stage renal disease: prevalence and patients characteristics of multiethnic population of United Arab Emirates" and reported that phosphate levels represented among more than half of the studied subjects and the researchers documented that the importance of treatment of hyperphosphatemia to reduce its negatively effect on the bone state.

Moreover, urea level among studied subjects in the current study was abnormal, this could be due to failure of the kidneys to excrete body waste products. This finding is supported with Nisha, SrinivasaKannan, Thanga-Mariappan & Jagatha, (2017) that they conducted a study titled "Biochemical evaluation of creatinine and urea in patients with renal failure undergoing hemodialysis", and reported that more than half of studied subjects complained high level of urea and reported that there was a complex relationship between urea and mortality in HD patients as patients with high or low urea levels exhibited higher mortality than those with medium levels.

Findings related to effectiveness of acupressure on insomnia and dizziness level:

Regarding to the first study hypothesis of the current study stated that, "Patients on hemodialysis who receive acupressure therapy will have lower mean insomnia scores than patients on hemodialysis who receive routine hospital care". Assessing the incidence of insomnia using the Insomnia Severity Index (ISI) questionnaire revealed that, studied patients on hemodialysis in both groups experiencing insomnia at the baseline assessment. This is supported by Hamzi et al., (2017) who expressed that the prevalence of clinically significant insomnia in HD patients is still high despite all the new technical and therapeutic advances of the last decade. Insomnia seems to be associated with long duration on dialysis in female gender. Also, Arache et al., (2019) who conducted a study in Morocco entitled "Poor quality of sleep in patients on chronic hemodialysis documented that the Insomnia is one of the most commonly reported in sleep disorders and represented among studied subjects and also they confirmed that early diagnosis is necessary to offer multidisciplinary care between nephrologists, psychiatrists, cardiologists, and neurologists.

Additionally, another study conducted by Lufiyani et al., (2019) entitled "Factors related to insomnia among end-stage renal disease patients on hemodialysis in Jakarta, Indonesia", as the researchers found that more than half of patients experiencing insomnia and depression is a common problem in patients undergoing HD and is associated with insomnia. Also, added that Intervention to decrease depression level is needed to improve the quality of sleep.

Another study conducted by Yildiz et al., (2016) entitled "Restless-legs syndrome and insomnia in hemodialysis patients" documented high prevalence of clinically significant insomnia among patients on hemodialysis. And the researchers reported that depression and insomnia are commonly found in patients undergoing HD. The same authors added that a close relationship among diabetes, depression, and insomnia and there were independent factors associated with insomnia severity were depression, older age and being under HD treatment. Additionally, Alkhuwaiter et al., 2020 indicated that the majority of the studied subjects reported insomnia and added that insomnia is frequently reported in patients undergoing HD and identification of cases of insomnia to start management will have a positive impact not only on the patient quality of life but also on the prognosis of the disease progression and minimize complications.

However, the level of insomnia was improved among the study group after completing six acupressure sessions as indicated by patients expressing satisfaction with the sleep pattern and decrease rate of insomnia severity. Moreover, this improvement continued until the 12 acupressure sessions that, the patients were very satisfied with the sleep pattern and had significant improvement in their quality of life and performing daily functioning.

Unlike the studied subjects in the control group who receiving routine hospital care, there was no observable improvement of insomnia level from baseline assessment to the final assessment; after four weeks. That, the majority of control group subjects continued to have moderate insomnia from baseline forward. Additionally, there was a high significant difference between study and control group in relation to insomnia level.

This finding could be explained by Nurul, Wiwik, Ika & Anna., (2018) who conveyed that acupressure improve sleep quality of patient on hemodialysis by releasing the neurological mediators to physical process; relaxes the muscles and encourages the body to relax, helps in releasing neuro-transmitter and serotonin that plays important role in synthesizing melatonin, thus reduces insomnia and increases the desire of sleep. Subsequently, the patients on hemodialysis in the study group fall easily in sleep after acupressure sessions.

Another study conducted by Kang & Kim, (2017) entitled "Effects of Acupressure on pruritus and sleep in patients on hemodialysis" and reported that, acupressure is an effective nursing intervention to increase the quality of sleep among patients undergoing HD. Additionally, another study conducted by Zeid & Aly, (2020) entitled "The Effect of Acupressure Technique on Sleep Quality among Patients Undergoing Hemodialysis" in Alexandria University, Egypt and the researchers expressed that the acupressure is an effective technique for promoting the sleep quality in patient on hemodialysis and its effect begins in overall sessions. Also added that post acupressure technique, the all sleep related problems decreased significantly in the studied subjects.

This technique may be the accumulative effect of acupressure for improving sleep disorders in patients on hemodialysis; especially those patients cannot take medications without restrictions. After implementation of twelve sessions of acupressure technique there was statistically significant differences between study and control groups. This was confirmed by the comparison of three quarters of their patients in the control group as patients under the study were complaining of severe insomnia comparing to less than one fifth of patients in the study group.

This might be attributed to the effect of mechanical pressure; acupressure has been known to decrease tissue adhesion, promote relaxation, increase regional blood circulation, increase parasympathetic nervous activity, increase intramuscular temperature, and decrease neuromuscular excitability. These findings suggested a good, safe, a noninvasive therapy and low expensive method for treatment of sleep disorders in hemodialysis patients. Training of this method is easy and it is applicable by nurses and patients (Zeid & Aly, 2020). Therefore, the first hypothesis of the current the study was supported.

Regarding the second hypothesis of the current study stated that "Patient on hemodialysis who receive acupressure therapy will have lower mean dizziness scores than those who receive routine hospital care". Assessing the incidence of dizziness using dizziness assessment tool revealed that studied patients on hemodialysis in both groups experiencing dizziness at baseline assessment. This is supported by Hintistan, & Deniz, (2018) who documented the high prevalence of clinically significant dizziness in patients on hemodialysis and reported that the frequency and severity of the dizziness experienced by patients receiving hemodialysis should be monitored regularly.

In addition, there was another study conducted by Zappia & Piccirillo, (2014) who expressed high prevalence of clinically significant dizziness in patients on hemodialysis and dizziness is considered as complication of HD, as it's negatively affect patients on hemodialysis. As well as, a study conducted by Chaiviboontham, Phinitkhajorndech & Tiansaard, (2020) entitled "Symptom clusters in patients with end-stage renal disease undergoing hemodialysis" and reported that the dizziness was expressed in nearly half of patients under the study and confirmed that patients undergoing hemodialysis should be routinely assessed regularly that reflected on the proper management resulting in enhancing patient's quality of life.

In relation to the effect of acupressure on dizziness in the current study, it was matched with a study conducted in Beni-Suef University, Egypt by Bayoumi, (2018) entitled "Implementation of Nursing Evidence -Based Practices in managing Interdialytic Hypotension during Hemodialysis Sessions: A Quasi-experimental study" as the researcher documented that the orthostatic hypotension and dizziness are more common reported among hemodialysis patients after a dialysis session. In the same line other study carried out by Polinder-Bos, Emmelot-Vonk, Gansevoort, Diepenbroek & Gaillard, (2014) entitled "High fall incidence and fracture rate in elderly dialysis patients" reported that around half of patients undergoing hemodialysis under study had an incidence of falls post-dialysis session.

Though, it is worth mentioning that, the level of dizziness was improved after completing six acupressure sessions as indicated by patient expressing satisfaction with decreasing symptoms of dizziness as lightheaded, nausea, drowsiness and feeling fainting. Moreover, this improvement continued until the 12 acupressure sessions that patients very satisfied with dizziness level and had significant improvement in the quality of life and performing daily functioning.

In the current study, there was no noticeable improvement of dizziness level among control group subjects - receiving routine hospital care - from baseline to the final assessment; after four weeks. That, the majority of control group subjects continued to have mild dizziness. Additionally, there was highly significant difference between study and control group in relation to dizziness level. This finding could be explained by Arun & Venkateshan, (2019) and documented that acupressure decrease dizziness symptoms, repair the energy flow, relax the body's organs. Therefore, the second hypothesis of the current study was supported.

Correlation findings

Concerning the relationship between insomnia and dizziness, the current study revealed that, there was a significant correlation between dizziness and insomnia among the study and control group subjects. This finding is in agreement with Kim, Kim, Jeon, & Hong, (2018) who conducted a study in Korea entitled " Relationship between sleep quality and dizziness and found that there was a strongly associations between sleep quality and dizziness. Therefore, it is important to consider sleep disturbance in patients on hemodialysis with dizziness and vice versa. Furthermore, findings depicted highly significant difference between study and control group subjects in relation to the variables of gender and nap time. These differences may help in explaining the former finding and some other research findings.

Also, the findings of the current study showed that effect of acupressure on insomnia and dizziness is effective in improving sleep quality of patient with hemodialysis, decrease dizziness symptoms, repair the energy flows, increase-releasing neuro-transmitter, neurohormon and serotonin, the previous effect can reduce insomnia and dizziness, relax the body's organs and increasing the desire of sleep and this finding supported by Nurul et al., (2018) and Arun & Venkateshan, (2019).

Moreover, the relation between insomnia and dizziness with associated diseases in the current study documented that, there was no significant correlation between insomnia and dizziness with associated diseases among the study and control group. This finding supported with study conducted by Bhaskar et al., (2016) in India entitled "Prevalence of chronic insomnia in adult patients and its correlation with medical comorbidities"

Several possible factors may have relevance to the observed phenomena of the improved level of sleep and dizziness among study group. One possible factor is patient's accepting complementary and alternative treatments due to its low cost; patient searching for means to avoid side effects and complication of medicine and out of despair from pharmacological management as this might be the final and last mean to save them from the pain and discomfort as the patients constantly suffering from. Also, old age plays important role in development insomnia and dizziness.

In conclusion, the current study could support the proposed hypothesis that patients on HD who receive the acupressure will have lower insomnia and dizziness level than those who don't.

Summary, Conclusion and Recommendations

This chapter summarizes the findings of the current study and suggests professional implications for nursing practice, patient education and research. Finally closes with recommendations for future study.

Summary

Chronic renal failure (CRF) is recognized as a major public health problem increasing worldwide. Chronic renal failure refers to irreversible renal dysfunction as manifested by the inability of the kidneys to excrete sufficient fluid and waste products from the body to maintain health (Abouna,2020) With progressive renal failure, glomerular filtration rate reduces below 15 ml/min in progressive renal failure leading to serious complications leading to death. All of these necessitate renal replacement therapy (RRT) alternate to RRT and constant timely hemodialysis (HD). Although hemodialysis is the most common methods to treat renal failure, the patients undergoing HD still have wide range of problems and complications such as dizziness and sleep disturbance (Hill et al., 2016)

Sleep disturbance is common in patients with end stage renal disease particularly on those undergoing dialysis therapies. One of the different forms of sleep disturbance is insomnia (Maung et al., 2016). Also dizziness is considered as a complication of HD and short term complication of insomnia (Medic et al., 2017). As a large consequence on patient quality of life, further impairing patients' daily functioning, motivation, social engagement, contributing to decrease in sleep quality and increased body pain. There is evidence to suggest that insomnia and dizziness may contribute directly to clinical outcomes, also increasing the risk of cardiac impairment and mortality. Hence, the need to assess and evaluate insomnia and dizziness level in patients undergoing dialysis is very important to patients' wellbeing and quality of life (Wanger, C. 2020).

A significant need exists for the management of insomnia and dizziness in order to reduce its impact on the life of patients undergoing HD for example improving their quality of life, perform their daily activities, improve their abilities or desires to spend time with other people decreasing sleeping problems and depression. Nurses are in a strategic position to assess dialysis-related insomnia and dizziness and help patients develop strategies to manage its effects. Recently, the use of complementary and alternative medicine has increased in conventional health care settings. Acupressure is commonly used for relaxation and to maintain a person's state of health. So, all health team should be following up all new modalities and alternative methods to reduce insomnia and dizziness level in HD patients (Yeung et al., 2018)

The aim of the current study is to evaluate the effect of acupressure therapy on insomnia and dizziness among patients undergoing hemodialysis. To fulfill the aim of this study the following research hypotheses were formulated: H_1: The study group patients who received acupressure therapy will have significant lower mean insomnia scores than control group who receive routine hospital care. H_2. The study group patients who received acupressure therapy will have significant lower mean dizziness scores than control group who receive routine hospital care.

A quasi-experimental time series design was utilized to achieve the purpose of this study. A nonprobability convenient consecutive sample consisting of 88 patients (44 in the experimental and 44 in the control group) admitted to Kasr El-Aini Center (Nephrology-Dialysis-Transplantation) at Cairo University hospital who accepted to participate in the study. Criteria for inclusion included male and female patients between 18-60 years old scheduled to undergo HD since more than three months ago and patients had insomnia and dizziness according to objective validated insomnia severity scale. Patients had congestive heart failure, cancer or suffering from itching and redness at the pressure points were excluded from the study.

Data was collected using the following three tools: (I) Structured Interview Questioner divided into two parts: (a) Demographic data (b) Medical Background data, (II) Insomnia Severity Index (ISI) and (III) Dizziness assessment tool. The first tool collected demographic and medical data pertinent to the study. The second tool consists of 7 questions concerning sleep pattern and sleep problems. Each item is marked on a 5-point Likert Scale (0 to 4) and the total score after evaluation ranged from 0 to 28. The third tool, this scale was developed by the investigator to assess dizziness severity symptom and consists of 15 questions and each item is scored on a ten-point Likert scale (zero to ten).

The Main Findings

The main findings of this study revealed that near half (45.5%) of the study group their age were 40 to 60 years old, around three quarter (72.7%) of the study group were females, the majority (90.9%) of them were living in urban areas, (29.5%) of the studied group had secondary education level, majority of them had no work (house wife or unemployed). While more than half of the study group was married.

Moreover, a meaningful reduction in the insomnia level among the study group; as insomnia mean score decreased from 16 at baseline to 12 after 6 sessions to 8 after 12 sessions. While in the control group remained nearly the same at the three times. Also, the current finding reported a noticeable reduction in the dizziness level in the study group as dizziness mean score decreased from 35 at baseline to 25 after 6 sessions to 12 after 12 sessions. While in the control group remained nearly the same at the three times. Additionally, there was statistical significant difference between insomnia and dizziness in the study and control group ($r = 0.55$, $P = 0.0001$ and $r = 0.56$, $P = 0.0001$) respectively.

Conclusion

Based on the current study findings the investigator concluded that:

Based on results of the current study, it can be concluded that insomnia and dizziness are common among majority of HD patients and have a significant impact on health status. With using acupressure therapy a significant reduction in the level of insomnia and dizziness was observed. The studied subjects found them comfortable and also expressed high level of satisfaction towards acupressure therapy. Also it is easy to be applied by nonprofessional caregiver or patients themselves. Thus without pharmacological intervention patients can use cheap and simple technique to relive insomnia and dizziness by improving sleep; relieve stress and tension; relax muscles and joints; minimize headache as well treat the symptoms of dizziness.

Recommendations

Upon the previous findings the following recommendations are suggested.

1. Replication of the study using larger probability sample from different geographical areas in Egypt.

2. Replication of the study matching subject on the variable of gender.

3. Use variable instruments of acupressure to reach the maximum deep pressure for points as sojuko and using of elbow for acupressure therapy.

4. Planning for education sessions for nursing team to raise awareness about the importance of acupressure for insomnia and dizziness and its importance in general.

5. Planning for acupressure course in the faculty of nursing and put additional part in curriculum of students about complementary health approach.

6. Illustrative booklet related to acupressure should be available to be known by all heath team members mainly nurses.

References

Abouna, A. M. (2020). Orofacial Manifestations of Chronic Renal Failure at Ahmed Gasim Center Hospital and Dr Salma for Kidney Diseases. Khartoum.

Aggarwal, H. K., Jain, D., Dabas, G., and Yadav, R. K. (2017). Prevalence of depression, anxiety and insomnia in chronic kidney disease patients and their co-relation with the demographic variables. Prilozi, 38(2), 35-44.

Ahmed, A. E., AL-Jahdali, H., Fatani, A., Al-Rouqi, K., AL-Jahdali, F., Al-Harbi, A., ... & Rumayyan, A.(2017). The effects of age and gender on the prevalence of insomnia in a sample of the Saudi population. Ethnicity & health, 22(3), 285-294.

Ali, E. A. E. G., Salem, Y. M., & Salem, M. A. (2015). Patients' satisfaction with nursing care in hemodialysis units. *Assiut Scientific Nursing Journal, 3*(6), 145-166.

Alkhuwaiter, R. S., Alsudais, R. A., & Ismail, A. A. (2020). A prospective study on prevalence and causes of insomnia among end-stage renal failure patients on hemodialysis in selected dialysis centers in Qassim, Saudi Arabia. *Saudi Journal of Kidney Diseases and Transplantation, 31*(2), 454.

Allah, E. S. A., Abdel-Aziz, H. R., & El-Seoud, A. R. A. (2014). Insomnia: prevalence, risk factors, and its effect on quality of life among elderly in Zagazig City, Egypt. Journal of nursing education and practice, 4(8), 52.

Allemand, L. D., Nóbrega, O. T., Lauar, J. P., Veiga, J. P. R., &Camargos, E. F. (2017). Sleep Parameters in Short Daily versus Conventional Dialysis: An Actigraphic Study. International journal of nephrology, 2017.

Arache, W., Laboudi, F., Ouanass, A., & El Kabbaj, D. (2019). Poor quality of sleep in patients on chronic hemodialysis. Ibnosina Journal of Medicine and Biomedical Sciences, 11(1) 20.

Arun, R. D., &Venkateshan, M. (2019).Effectiveness of acupressure on quality of sleep of hemodialysis patients. International Journal of Nursing Education, 11(1),60-66.

Bayoumi, M. (2018). Implementation of Nursing Evidence-Based Practices in managing Interdialytic Hypotension during Hemodialysis sessions: A Quasi-experimental study.

Benarroch, E. E. (2019). Control of the cardiovascular and respiratory systems during sleep. Autonomic Neuroscience, 218, 54-63.

Best Effective Acupressure Points for Sleeping Disorders (2017). *Available @https: // acupressurepointsguide. com/acupressure-points-for-sleeping-disorders/.*

Bhaskar, S., Hemavathy, D., & Prasad, S. (2016). Prevalence of chronic insomnia in adult patients and its correlation with medical comorbidities. *Journal of family medicine and primary care, 5*(4), 780.

Blumberg, M. S., Lesku, J. A., Libourel, P. A., Schmidt, M. H., & Rattenborg, N. C. (2020). What Is REM Sleep?. *Current Biology, 30*(1), R38-R49

.

Bossola, M., Di Stasio, E., Antocicco, M., Pepe, G., Marzetti, E., &Vulpio, C. (2017). 1-year course of fatigue in patients on chronic hemodialysis. International urology and nephrology, 1-8.

Brinkman, J. E., & Sharma, S. (2019). Physiology, sleep. In StatPearls [Internet].StatPearls Publishing.

Carley, D. W., & Farabi, S. S. (2016). Physiology of sleep. *Diabetes Spectrum, 29*(1),5-9.

Centers for Disease Control and Prevention. Chronic Kidney Disease Surveillance System Accessed January 7, 2019.

Chaiviboontham, S., Phinitkhajorndech, N., & Tiansaard, J. (2020). Symptom Clusters in Patients with End-Stage Renal Disease Undergoing Hemodialysis. *International Journal of Nephrology and Renovascular Disease, 13*, 297.

Chalmers, Charlotte. (2019). Applied anatomy and physiology and the renal disease process. *Renal Nursing: Care and Management of People with Kidney Disease*, 21-58.

Chalouhy, C.E., (2017). Kidney Anatomy. Available @ https://emedicine.medscape.com/article/1948775-overview.

Chang, T. I., Zheng, Y., Montez-Rath, M. E., &Winkelmayer, W. C. (2016).Antihypertensive medication use in older patients transitioning from chronic kidney disease to end-stage renal disease on dialysis. *Clinical Journal of the American Society of Nephrology, 11*(8), 1401-1412.

Chatfield, C. (2016). The analysis of time series: an introduction. CRC press. Available *@https://books.google.com/books/about/The_Analysis_of_Time_Series.html?id=q KzyAbdaDFAC*

Chen, T. K., Knicely, D. H., & Grams, M. E. (2019). Chronic kidney disease diagnosis and management: a review. Jama, 322(13), 1294-1304.

Chokroverty & Ferini-Strambi, (2017). Physiological changes of sleep. In Sleep Disorders Medicine (pp. 153-194). Springer, New York, NY.

Chu, G., Szymanski, K., Tomlins, M., Yates, N., & McDonald, V. M. (2018). Nursing care considerations for dialysis patients with a sleep disorder. *Renal Society of Australasia Journal, 14*(2).

Crisler, Johnston, Sivula & Budelsky (2020). Functional Anatomy and Physiology. In The Laboratory Rat (pp. 91-132). Academic Press. available @https://www. google .com /search?q= frontal section of right kidney.

Danielle, F. M. E. H., Mahamat, M., Francois, K. F., Marie-Patrice, H., & Gloria, A. (2017). Sleep Quality on Maintenance Hemodialysis Patients in Douala General Hospital in Cameroon. OpenJournal of Nephrology, 7(03), 61.

Delaney, Kowalewska, & Treuting, (2018). Urinary System. In Comparative Anatomy and Histology (pp. 275-301). Academic Press. Available @https://www. google .com /search?q = structures of the human urinary system .

Dijk, D. J., Beersma, D. G., van den Hoofdakker, R. H., Duffy, J. F., Kiel, E., Shanahan, T. L., & Czeisler, C. A. (2019). Sleep deprivation: An unmet public health problem. Washington, DC: Institute of Medicine: National Academies Press. https://doi. org. Handbook of Sleep Research, 30, 178.

Doenges, M. E., Moorhouse, M. F., & Murr, A. C. (2019). Nursing care plans: Guidelines for individualizing client care across the life span. FA Davis.

Dyhrfjeld-Johnsen, J., & Attali, P. (2019). Management of peripheral vertigo with antihistamines: New options on the horizon. British journal of clinical pharmacology, 85(10), 2255-2263.

El-Arbagy, A. R., Yassin, Y. S., & Boshra, B. N. (2016). Study of prevalence of end-stage renal disease in Assiut governorate, upper Egypt. Menoufia Medical Journal, 29(2).

Fairweather, J., Findlay, M., & Isles, C. (2020). Overview of Chronic Kidney Disease. In Clinical Companion in Nephrology (pp. 119-124). Springer, Cham., Available@https://phacdochuabenh.com/Clinical-Medicine/ 88 .php.

Fluck, R. (2016). Intensive Hemodialysis and Treatment Complications and Tolerability.

Flythe, J. E., Hilliard, T., Lumby, E., Castillo, G., Orazi, J., Abdel-Rahman, E. M., ...& Wilkie, C. M. (2018). Fostering Innovation in Symptom Management among Hemodialysis Patients: Paths Forward for Insomnia, Muscle Cramps, and Fatigue. Clinical Journal of the American Society of Nephrology, CJN-07670618.

Fraenkel, P. G. (2015). Understanding anemia of chronic disease. ASH Education Program Book, 2015(1), 14-18.

Fountain, J. H., & Lappin, S. L. (2017). Physiology, renin angiotensin system.

Gerretsen, P., Shah, P., Logotheti, A., Attia, M., Balakumar, T., Sulway, S., ...& Rutka, J. A. (2019). Interdisciplinary integration of nursing and psychiatry (INaP) for the treatment of dizziness. The Laryngoscope.

Ghonemy, T. A., Farag, S. E., Soliman, S. A., El-Okely, A., and El-Hendy, Y. (2016). Epidemiology and risk factors of chronic kidney disease in the El-Sharkia Governorate, Egypt. *Saudi Journal of Kidney Diseases and Transplantation, 27(1),* 111.

Gilan, N., Naseem, E., & Mohamed, E. (2018). Role of Erythropoietin in Renal failure.

Goldberg, I., & Krause, I. (2016). The role of gender in Chronic Kidney Disease. EMJ, 1(2), 58-64.

Goyal, A., & Singh, S. (2020). Hypocalcemia. *StatPearls [Internet].*

Grima, N. A., Bei, B., & Mansfield, D. (2019). Insomnia management. *Australian Journal of General Practice, 48(4),* 198.

Hall, H., Leach, M., Brosnan, C., & Collins, M. (2017). Nurses' attitudes towards complementary therapies: A systematic review and meta-synthesis. *International journal of nursing studies, 69*, 47-56.

Hamzi, M. A., Hassani, K., Asseraji, M., & El Kabbaj, D. (2017). Insomnia in hemodialysis patients: A multicenter study from morocco. Saudi Journal of Kidney Diseases and Transplantation, 28(5), 1112.

Hare J, Clark-Carter D, Forshaw M. (2014). A randomized controlled trial to evaluate the effectiveness of a cognitive behavioural group approach to improve patient adherence to peritoneal dialysis fluid restrictions: a Pilot study. Nephrol Dial Transplant, 29: 555–564.

Hasegawa, T., Koiwa, F., &Akizawa, T. (2018). Anemia in conventional hemodialysis: Finding the optimal treatment balance. In *Seminars in Dialysis* (Vol. 31, No. 6, pp. 599-606).

Hill, N. R., Fatoba, S. T., Oke, J. L., Hirst, J. A., O'Callaghan, C. A., Lasserson, D. S., & Hobbs, F. R. (2016). Global prevalence of chronic kidney disease–a systematic review and meta-analysis. *PloS one, 11*(7), e015876.

Hintistan, S., & Deniz, A. (2018). Evaluation of symptoms in patients undergoing hemodialysis. *Bezmialem Science*, *6*, 112-118.

Ibrahim, J., Hazzan, A. D., Mathew, A. T., Sakhiya, V., Zhang, M., Halinski, C., & Fishbane, S. (2018). Medication discrepancies in late-stage chronic kidney disease. Clinical kidney journal, 11(4), 507-512.

Javaheri, S., & Redline, S. (2017). Insomnia and risk of cardiovascular disease. *Chest*, *152*(2), 435-444.

Jawabri, K. H., & Raja, A. (2020). Physiology, Sleep Patterns. *StatPearls [Internet]*.

Jbireal, J. M., Azab, A. E., & Omer, I. S. K. (2020).Variation of Hematological Parameters in Renal Failure and Hemodialysis Patients.

John, A. S., Mboto, C. I., & Agbo, B. (2016). A review on the prevalence and predisposing factors responsible for urinary tract infection among adults. *Euro J Exp Bio*, *6*(4), 7-11.

Kallenbach, J. Z. (2020). *Review of hemodialysis for nurses and dialysis personnel-e-book*. Elsevier health sciences. Available @https:/ /www. niddk.nih.gov/health-information/kidney-disease/kidney-failure/hemodialysis

Kang, M., & Kim, Y. K. (2017). Effects of acupressure on pruritus and sleep in patients on hemodialysis. *Journal of Korean Academy of Fundamentals of Nursing, 24*(1), 9-17.

Kasr Al - Aini Hospital Medical Records and Statistics Department, Cairo University. (2019).

Kesser, B. W., & Gleason, A. T. (2018). Dizziness and vertigo across the lifespan. Elsevier Health Sciences.

Koketsu, J. S. (2017). Sleep and rest. Pedretti's Occupational Therapy-E-Book: Practice Skills for Physical Dysfunction, 305.

Kim, S. K., Kim, J. H., Jeon, S. S., & Hong, S. M. (2018). Relationship between sleep quality and dizziness. PloS one, 13(3).

Kumar, B. K., &Sagar, R. (2019). A study of sleep quality and its correlates in end-stage renal disease patients on hemodialysis. Open Journal of Psychiatry& Allied Sciences,10(1)9-14.

Lam, W. C., Zhong, L., Liu, Y., Shi, N., Ng, B., Ziea, E., ...& Lu, A. (2019). Hong Kong Chinese medicine clinical practice guideline for cancer palliative care: pain, constipation, and insomnia. *Evidence-Based Complementary and Alternative Medicine, 2019.*

Lenggogeni, D. P., Sitorus, R., & Maria, R. (2019). Sleep Quality among Hemodialysis Patients. In *Enhancing Capacity of Healthcare Scholars and professionals in Responding to the Global Health Issues* (pp. 63-69).Sciendo.

Leschziner, Guy. D. (2018). Restless legs syndrome. In *Sleep Disorders in Psychiatric Patients* (pp. 175-188). Springer, Berlin, Heidelberg.

Lovato, N., & Lack, L. (2019). Insomnia and mortality: a meta-analysis. *Sleep Medicine Reviews, 43,* 71-83.

Lufiyani, I., Zahra, A. N.,& Yona, S. (2019). Factors related to insomnia among end-stage renal disease patients on hemodialysis in Jakarta, Indonesia. Enfermeriaclinica, 29,331-335.

Mahmoud, M. M., AboZead, S. E., Mohammad, W. H., El-all, A., &ElRazik, H. A. (2019). Assessment Quality of Sleep in Patients undergoing Hemodialysis. *Assiut Scientific Nursing Journal, 7*(17), 74-80.

Makris, K., & Spanou, L. (2016). Acute kidney injury: definition, pathophysiology and clinical phenotypes. *The Clinical Biochemist Reviews, 37*(2), 85.

Mashkoor, A. (2016). The hemodialysis machine case study.In *International Conference on Abstract State Machines, Alloy, B, TLA, VDM, and Z* (pp. 329-343). Springer, Cham.

Maung, S. C., El Sara, A., Chapman, C., Cohen, D., & Cukor, D. (2016). Sleep disorders and chronic kidney disease. World journal of nephrology, 5(3), 224.

Medic, G., Wille, M., & Hemels, M. E. (2017). Short-and long-term health consequences of sleep disruption. Nature and Science of Sleep, 9, 151.

Mehta, P., Dhapte, V., Kadam, S., & Dhapte, V. (2017). Contemporary acupressure therapy: Adroit cure for painless recovery of therapeutic ailments. Journal of traditional and complementary.

Mehta, P., Dhapte, V., Kadam, S., & Dhapte, V. (2017).Available @https://www.sciencedirect.com.

Michał, W., Grzegorz, L., Karol, C., Tadeusz, K., Magdalena, N., &Bartosz, M. (2020). Anemia of Chronic Diseases: Wider Diagnostics-Better Treatment?. *Nutrients, 12*(6), E1784.

Miller, K. E., & Gehrman, P. R. (2019). REM Sleep: What Is It Good For?. *Current Biology, 29*(16), R806-R807.

National Institute of Diabetes and Digestive and Kidney Diseases. Kidney Failure. Retrieved 11 November 2017.

Nsha, R., SrinivasaKannan, S. R., ThangaMariappan, K., &Jagatha, P. (2017). Biochemical evaluation of creatinine and urea in patients with renal failure undergoing hemodialysis. *J Clin Path Lab Med, 1*(2), 1-5.

Nobahar, M. (2017). Exploring medicine, 7(2), 251-263.experiences of the quality of nursing care among patients, nurses, caregivers and physicians in a haemodialysis department. Journal of renal care, 43(1), 50-59.

NoroziFiroz, M., Shafipour, V., Jafari, H., Hosseini, S. H., &Yazdani-Charati, J. (2019). Relationship of Hemodialysis Shift With Sleep Quality and Depression in Hemodialysis Patients. Clinical nursing research, 28(3), 356-373.

Nurul, h., Wiwik, u., Ika, p. s., & Anna, r. (2018). shenmen, neiguan and yongquan acupoints to improving sleep quality of hemodialysis patients: systematic review.

Ostermann, M., & Joannidis, M. (2016). Acute kidney injury 2016: diagnosis and diagnostic workup. Critical care, 20(1), 299.

Park, J. H., & Lee, H. J. (2019). Clinical Nurses' Knowledge and EducationalNeeds about Dizziness. J Korean BiolNursSci, 21(4), 259.

Patel, A. K., & Araujo, J. F. (2018). Physiology, sleep stages. In *StatPearls [Internet]*. StatPearls Publishing.

Pfieffer, M. L., Anthamatten, A., & Glassford, M. (2019). Assessment and treatment of dizziness and vertigo. The Nurse Practitioner, 44(10), 29-36.

Pinheiro, R. L., de Macedo, B. M., & de Carvalho Lira, A. L. B. (2017). Complications in patients with chronic renal failure undergoing hemodialysis. CogitareEnferm, 22(4), e52907.

Polinder-Bos, H. A., Emmelot-Vonk, M. H., Gansevoort, R. T., Diepenbroek, A., & Gaillard, C. A. (2014). High fall incidence and fracture rate in elderly dialysis patients. *Neth J Med, 72*(10), 509-515.

Rabbani, S. A., SB, S., &Rao, P. G. (2017). Hyperphosphatemia in end stage renal disease: prevalence and patients characteristics of multiethnic population of United Arab Emirates. Int J Pharm PharmSci, 9, 283.

Richards, C. (2016). Nephrology nursing and education. Nephrology Nursing Journal, 43(2), 93-95.

Sachdeva, J. (2019). Sleep Disorders in Chronic Pain. In *Pain* (pp. 421-423). Springer, Cham.

Sattar, S., Khan, N., Ahmad, F., Adnan, F., & Danish, S. H. (2016). Post-dialysis effects in patients on haemodialysis. JPMA. The Journal of the Pakistan Medical Association, 66(6), 781-788.

Scanlon, V. C., & Sanders, T. (2018). Essentials of anatomy and physiology. FA Davis.

Shim, H. Y., & Cho, M. K. (2017). Factors Influencing the Quality of Life of Hemodialysis Patients according to Symptom Cluster. Journal of CliniclNursing.

Taha, N.M., and Ali, Z.H. (2015). Can A Nursing Intervention Improve the Sleep Pattern Disorders in Patients Undergoing Hemodialysis in Morning and Afternoon Shifts? *Journal of Nursing and Care. Mar 12*, 2015.

Terrill, B. (2016). Renal nursing: a guide to practice. Routledge.

Thakral, M., Von Korff, M., McCurry, S. M., Morin, C. M., & Vitiello, M. V. (2020). ISI-3: Evaluation of a brief screening tool for insomnia. Sleep Medicine.

Thomas, S. J., & Calhoun, D. (2017). Sleep, insomnia, and hypertension: current findings and future directions. *Journal of the American Society of Hypertension, 11*(2), 122-129.

Thongprayoon, C., Acharya, P., Acharya, C., Chenbhanich, J., Bathini, T., Boonpheng, B & Cheungpasitporn, W. (2018). Hypocalcemia and bone mineral density changes following denosumab treatment in end-stage renal disease patients: a meta-analysis of observational studies. Osteoporosis International, 29(8), 1737-1745.

Tubbs, A. S., Dollish, H. K., Fernandez, F., & Grandner, M. A. (2019).The basics of sleep physiology and behavior.In Sleep and health (pp. 3-10).Academic Press.

Wagner, C. (2020). Complementary and alternative medicine. The United States Healthcare System: Overview, Driving Forces, and Outlook for the Future. Chicago, IL: Health Administration Press.

Waits, A., Tang, Y. R., Cheng, H. M., Tai, C. J., & Chien, L. Y. (2018). Acupressure effect on sleep quality: a systematic review and meta-analysis. *Sleep medicine reviews, 37*, 24-34.

Wang, J., Yue, P., Huang, J., Xie, X., Ling, Y., Jia, L., ...& Sun, F. (2018). Nursing intervention on the compliance of hemodialysis patients with end-stage renal disease: a meta-analysis. Blood purification, 45(1-3), 102-109.

Wang, R., Tang, C., Chen, X., Zhu, C., Feng, W., Li, P., & Lu, C. (2016). Poor sleep and reduced quality of life were associated with symptom distress in patients receiving maintenance hemodialysis. *Health and quality of life outcomes*, *14*(1), 125.

Wang, Y. P., & Hou, X. S. (2019). Discussion on the Classification of Acupoints. Zhongguozhenjiu= Chinese acupuncture & moxibustion, 39(10), 1069-1072.

Webster, A. C., Nagler, E. V., Morton, R. L., & Masson, P. (2017). Chronic kidney disease. The lancet, 389(10075), 1238-1252.

Wichniak, A., Wierzbicka, A., Walęcka, M., & Jernajczyk, W. (2017). Effects of antidepressants on sleep. *Current psychiatry reports*, *19*(9), 63.

Wingerd, B., & Taylor, P. B. (2020). The human body: Concepts of anatomy and physiology. Jones & Bartlett Publishers.

Yayan, J., Rasche, K., & Vlachou, A. (2017). Obstructive sleep apnea and chronic kidney disease. In *Clinical Management of Pulmonary Disorders and Diseases* (pp. 11-18).Springer, Cham.

Yeung, W. F., Ho, F. Y. Y., Chung, K. F., Zhang, Z. J., Yu, B. Y. M., Suen, L. K. P., ... & Lao, L. X. (2018). Self-administered acupressure for insomnia disorder: a pilot randomized controlled trial. Journal of Sleep , 27(2), 220-231.

Yildiz, D., Kahvecioğlu, S., Buyukkoyuncu, N., Kilic, A. K., Yildiz, A., Gul, C. B., ...& Tufan, F. (2016). Restless-legs syndrome and insomnia in hemodialysis patients. Renal failure, 38(2), 194-197.

Yuejuan, W., Biyan, Z., Youbao, L., Xianhui, Q., Binyan, W., Xin, X., Xiping, X. (2017). Relationship of diabetes with renal dysfunction in hypertensive adults. *Medicine: June2017-96-24*-e7169doi:10.1097/MD.7169.

Zeid, N. A. M., & Aly, S. E. B. (2020). The Effect of Acupressure Technique on Sleep Quality among Patients Undergoing Hemodialysis.

Zappia, C. P., & Piccirillo, B. (2014). Ataxia and dizziness in a patient on hemodialysis. Journal of the American Academy of PAs, 27(12), 56-58.

Contents

I want morebooks!

Buy your books fast and straightforward online - at one of world's fastest growing online book stores! Environmentally sound due to Print-on-Demand technologies.

Buy your books online at
www.morebooks.shop

Kaufen Sie Ihre Bücher schnell und unkompliziert online – auf einer der am schnellsten wachsenden Buchhandelsplattformen weltweit! Dank Print-On-Demand umwelt- und ressourcenschonend produziert.

Bücher schneller online kaufen
www.morebooks.shop

Printed by Books on Demand GmbH, Norderstedt / Germany